LIFE TOGETHER STUDENT EDITION

SURRENDERING

YOUR LIFE TO HONOR GOD

LIFE TOGETHER STUDENT EDITION

SURRENDERING

YOUR LIFE TO HONOR GOD

6 small group sessions
on worship

Doug Fields &
Brett Eastman

SURRENDERING Your Life to Honor God: 6 Small Group Sessions on Worship

Copyright© 2003 by Doug Fields and Lifetogether™

Youth Specialties Books,300 South Pierce Street, El Cajon, CA 92020, are published by Zondervan, 5300 Patterson Southeast, Grand Rapids MI 49530

Library of Congress Cataloging-in-Publication Data

Fields, Doug, 1962-
   Surrendering your life to honor God : 6 small group sessions on
worship / by Doug Fields and Brett Eastman.
          p. cm.
Summary: Presents lessons to be used by small groups to explore ways of
worshiping God through prayer, fellowship, and ministry, as well as
throughout one's daily life.
   ISBN 0-310-25338-1 (pbk.)
   1. Christian teenagers--Religious life--Juvenile literature. 2.
Worship--Juvenile literature. [1. Worship. 2. Christian life. 3.
Teenagers--Religious life.] I. Eastman, Brett, 1959- II. Title.
   BV4531.3.F545 2003
   259'.23--dc21
                                              2003005876

Concept and portions of this curriculum are from Doing Life Together (Zondervan, 2002), used by per-mission from Brett & Dee Eastman, Karen Lee-Thorp and Denise & Todd Wendorff.

Editorial and Art Direction: Rick Marschall
Production Coordinator: Nicole Davis
Edited: Vicki Newby
Cover and interior design: Tyler Mattson, NomadicMedia.net
Interior layouts, design management, production: Mark Rayburn, RayburnDesign.com
Proofreading: Vicki Newby and Linnea Lagerquist
Design Assistance: Katherine Spencer
Production Assistance: Roni Meek, Amy Aecovalle
Author photos: Brian Wiertzema and Art Zipple

Printed in the United States of America

05 06 07 08 09 // 10 9 8 7 6

ACKNOWLEDGMENTS

I'm thankful to the adult volunteers at Saddleback Church who are great small group leaders and to the students who are growing spiritually because they're connected to other believers. Good things are happening, and I'm so proud of you!

I'm thankful to the team at www.simplyyouthministry.com for working so hard to help create these types of resources that assist youth ministers and students throughout the world.

Gratitude for help on this project goes to Dennis Beckner, Kathleen Hamer, Erica Hamer, and especially Matt McGill who read every word of each book in the series and has made a big difference in my life and the books I write. What a joy to do life together with friends!

—DF

CONTENTS

Welcome to a relational journey!

My prayer is that this book, a few friends, and a loving adult leader will take you on a journey that will revolutionize your life. The following six sessions were designed to help you grow as a Christian in the context of a caring, spiritual community. This community is a group of people committed to doing life together, at least for a season of your life. Spiritual community is formed when each small group member focuses on Jesus and the others in the group.

Creating spiritual community isn't easy. It requires trust, confidentiality, honesty, care, and commitment to meet regularly with your group. These are rare qualities in today's world. Any two or three people can meet together and call it a group, but it takes something special from you to create a community in which you can be known, be loved, be cared for, and feel safe enough to reveal thoughts, doubts, and struggles and still to be yourself. You may be tempted to show up at the small group session and sit, smile, and be nice, but never speak from your heart or say anything that would challenge another group member's thinking. This type of superficial participation prevents true spiritual community.

Most relationships never get beneath the relational surface. This LIFETOGETHER series is designed to push you to think, to talk, and to open your heart. You'll be challenged to expose some of your fears, hurts, and habits. As you do this, you'll find healing, experience spiritual growth, and build lasting, genuine friendships. Since God uses people to impact people you'll most likely become a richer, deeper, more vibrant person as you experience LIFETOGETHER with others. If you go through this book (and the 5 other books in this series) you will become a deeper and stronger follower of Jesus Christ. Get ready for something big to happen in your life!

WHAT YOU'LL FIND IN EACH SESSION

For each session, the group time contains five sections, one for each of the primary biblical purposes: fellowship, discipleship, ministry, evangelism, and worship. The five purposes can each stand alone, but when they're fused together, they make a greater impact on you and your world than the five of them might if approached separately. Think about it like this: If you play baseball or softball, you might be an outstanding hitter, but you also need to be able to catch, throw, run, and slide. You need more than one skill to make an impact for your team. In the same way, the five purposes individually are good, but when you put them all together, you're a balanced player who makes a huge impact.

The material in this book (and the other LIFETOGETHER books) is built around God's Word. You'll find a lot of blank spaces and journaling pages where you can write down your thoughts about God's work in your life as you explore and live out God's purposes.

Here's a closer look at what you'll find in these five sections:

FELLOWSHIP: CONNECTING Your Heart to Others'
[goal: to have students share about their lives and listen attentively to others]

These questions give you and the members of your small group a chance to share from your own lives, to get to know one another better, and to offer initial thoughts on the session theme. The picture for this section is a heart because you're opening up your heart so others can connect with you on a deeper level.

DISCIPLESHIP: GROWING to Be Like Jesus
[goal: to explore God's Word, learn biblical knowledge, and make personal applications]

This is the time to explore the Bible, gain biblical knowledge, and discuss how God's Word can make a difference in your life. The picture for this section is a brain because you're opening your mind to learn God's Word and ways.

You'll find lots of questions in this section; more than you can discuss during your group time. Your leader will choose the questions your group will discuss. You can respond to the other questions on your own during the week, which is a great way to get more Bible study. (See **At Home This Week** on page 28.)

MINISTRY: SERVING Others in Love
[goal: to recognize and take opportunities to serve others]

During each small group session, you'll have an opportunity to discuss how to meet needs by serving others. As you grow spiritually, you'll begin to recognize—and take—opportunities to serve others. As your heart expands, so will your opportunities to serve. Here, the picture is a foot because you're moving your feet to meet the needs of others.

EVANGELISM: SHARING Your Story and God's Story
[goal: to consider how the truths from this lesson might be applied to our relationships with unbelievers]

It's too easy for a small group to become a clique and only care about one another. That's not God's plan for us. He wants us to reach out to people with the good news. Each session will give you an opportunity to discuss your relationships with unbelievers and consider ways to reach out to them. The picture for this section is a mouth because you're opening your mouth to have spiritual conversations with unbelievers.

WORSHIP: SURRENDERING Your Life to Honor God
[goal: to focus on God's presence]

Each small group session ends with a time of prayer. You'll be challenged to slow down and turn your focus toward God's love, his goodness, and his presence in your life. You'll spend time talking to God, listening in silence, and giving your heart to him. Surrender is giving up what you want so God can give you what he wants. The picture for this section is a body, which represents you surrendering your entire life to God.

AT HOME THIS WEEK

At the end of each session, you'll find reminders of ways you can help yourself grow spiritually until your small group meets again. You're free to vary the options you choose from week to week. You'll find more information about each of these options near the end of the first session.

Daily Bible Readings

Page 104 contains a list of Bible passages to help you continue to take God's Word deeper in your life.

Memory Verses

On page 108 you'll find six Bible verses to memorize, one related to the topic of each session.

Journaling

You're offered several options to trigger your thoughts, including a question or two related to the topic of the session. Journaling is a great way to reflect on what you've been learning or to evaluate it. **"SCRIBBLES"** journaling page are on page 113-125.

Wrap It Up

Each session contains a lot of discussion questions, too many for one small group meeting. So you can think through your answers to the extra questions during the week.

LEARN A LITTLE MORE

You might want to learn a little more (hey, great title for a subsection!) about terms and phrases in the Bible passage. You'll find helpful information here.

FOR FURTHER STUDY

One of the best ways to understand Bible passages is by reading other verses on the same topic. You'll find suggestions here.

BEING IN A SMALL GROUP

You probably have enough casual or superficial friendships and don't need to waste your time cultivating more. To benefit the most from your small group time and to build great relationships, here are some ideas to help you:

Prepare to participate

Interaction is a key to a good small group. Talking too little will make it hard for others to get to know you. Everyone has something to contribute—yes, even you! But participating doesn't mean dominating, so be careful to not monopolize the conversation! Most groups typically have one conversation hog, and if you don't know who it is in your small group, then it might be you. Here's a tip: you don't have to answer every question and comment on every point. The bottom line is to find a balance between the two extremes.

Be consistent

Healthy relationships take time to grow. Quality time is great, but a great *quantity* of time is probably better. Plan to show up every week (or whenever your group plans to meet), even when you don't feel like it. With only six sessions per book, if you miss just two meetings you'll have missed 33 percent of the small group times for this book. When you make a commitment to your small group a high priority, you're sure to build meaningful relationships.

Practice honesty and confidentiality

Strong relationships are only as solid as the trust they are built upon. Although it may be difficult, take a risk and be honest with your answers. God wants you to be known by others! Then respect the risks others are taking and offer them the same love, grace, and forgiveness God does. Make confidentiality a nonnegotiable value for your small group. Nothing kills community like gossip.

Come prepared

You can always arrive prepared by praying ahead of time. Ask God to give you the courage to be honest and the discipline to be respectful of others.

You aren't required to do any preparation in the workbook before you arrive (unless you're the leader—and then it's just a few minutes). But you may want to work through the **Growing** questions before your group time. Talk about this idea with your leader. If your group is going to do this, don't view the preparation as homework but as an opportunity to learn more about yourself and God to prepare yourself to go deeper.

Congratulations...

...on making a commitment to go through this material with your small group! Life change is within reach when people are united through the same commitment. Your participation in a small group can have a lasting and powerful impact on your life. Our prayer is that the questions and activities in this book help you grow closer to the other group members, and more importantly, to grow closer to God.

Doug Fields & Brett Eastman

Doug and Brett were part of the same small group for several years. Brett was the pastor of small groups at Saddleback Church where Doug is the pastor to students. Brett and a team of friends wrote Doing LifeTogether, a group study for adults. Everyone loved it so much that they asked Doug to revise it for students. So even though Brett and Doug both had a hand in this book, it's written as though Doug were sitting with you in your small group. For more on Doug and Brett see page 144.

FOR SMALL GROUP LEADERS

As the leader, prepare yourself by reading through the lesson and thinking about how you might lead it. The questions are a guide for you to help students grow spiritually. Think through which questions are best for your group. No curriculum author knows your students better than you. This small amount of preparation will help you manage the time you'll have together.

How to Go through Each Lesson

This book was written to be more like a guidebook than a workbook. In most workbooks, you're supposed to answer every question and fill in all the blanks. In this book, there are lots of questions and plenty of space.

Rule number one is that there are no rules about how you must go through the material. Every small group is unique and will figure out its own style and system. (The exception is when the lead youth worker establishes a guideline for all the groups to follow. In that case, respect your leader and conform your group to the leader's guidelines).

If you need a standard to get you started until you navigate your own way, this is how we used the material for a 60-minute session.

Intro (4 minutes)
Begin each session with one student reading the **Small Group Covenant** (see page 88). This becomes a constant reminder of why you're doing what you're doing. Then have another student read the opening paragraphs of the session you'll be discussing. Allow different students to take turns reading these two opening pieces.

Connecting (10 minutes)
This section can take 45 minutes if you're not careful to manage the time. You'll need to lead to keep this segment short. Consider giving students a specific amount of time and hold them to it. It's always better to leave students wanting more time for an activity than to leave them tired and bored.

Growing (25 minutes)
Read God's Word and work through the questions you think will be best for your group. This section will usually have more questions than you are able to discuss. Before the small group begins, take time to read through the questions to choose the best ones for your group. You may want to add questions of your own.

Serving and Sharing (10 minutes)
We typically choose one of these two sections to skip if pressed for time. If you decide to skip one or the other, group members can finish the section on their own during the week. Don't feel guilty about passing over a section. One of the strengths of this material is the built-in, intentional repetition. You'll have other opportunities to discuss that biblical purpose.

Surrendering (10 minutes)
We always want to end the lesson with a focus on God and a specific time of prayer. You'll be given several options, but you can always default to your group's comfort level to finish your time.

Closing Challenge (1 minute)
We encourage the students to pick one option from the **At Home This Week** section

that they'll do on their own. The more often students are able to take the initiative and develop the habit of spending time with God, the healthier they will be in their spiritual journey. We've found that students have plenty of unanswered questions that they want to go back and consider on their own.

Keep in Mind

- The main goal of this book isn't to have group members answer every question. The goal is **spiritual growth.**
- Make whatever adjustments you think are necessary.
- It's your small group, it's your time, and the questions will always be there. Use them, ignore them, or assign them to be answered during the week.
- Don't feel the pressure to have everyone answer every question.
- Questions are a great way to get students connecting to one another and God's Word.

Suggestions for Existing Small Groups

If your small group has been meeting for a while and you've already established comfortable relationships, you can jump right into the material. Make sure you take the following actions, even if you're a well-established group:

- Read through the **Small Group Covenant** on page 88 and make additions or adjustments.
- Read the **Prayer Request Guidelines** together (on page 128). You can maximize the group's time by following these guidelines.
- Consider whether you're going to assign the material to be completed (or at least thought through) before each meeting.
- Familiarize yourself with all the **At Home This Week** options that follow each lesson. They are detailed near the end of Session 1 (page 28) and summarized after the other five lessons.

Although handling business like this can seem cumbersome or unnecessary to an existing group, these foundational steps can save you from headaches later because you took the time to create an environment conducive to establishing deep relationships.

Suggestions for New Small Groups

If your group is meeting together for the first time, jumping right into the first lesson may not be your best option. You might want to have a meeting before you begin going through the book so you can get to know each other. To prepare for the first gathering, read and follow the **Suggestions for Existing Groups.**

When you get together with your group members, spend time getting to know one another by using ice-breaker questions. Several are listed here. Pick one or two that will work best for your group. Or you may have ice breakers of your own that you'd like to use. The goal is to break ground in order to plant the seeds of healthy relationships.

Ice Breakers

1. What's your name, school, grade, and favorite class in school? (Picking your least favorite class is too easy.)

2. Tell the group a brief (basic) history of your family. What's your family life like? How many brothers and sisters do you have? Which family members are you closest to?

3. What's one thing about yourself that you really like?

4. Everyone has little personality quirks—strange and unique habits that other people usually laugh about. What are yours?

5. Why did you choose to be a part of this small group?

6. What do you hope to get out of this small group? How do you expect it to help you?

7. In your opinion, what do you think it will take to make our small group work?

Great resources are available to help you!

Companion DVDs are available for the LifeTogether small group books. These DVDs contain teaching segments you can use to supplement each session by playing them before your small group discussion begins or just prior to the Growing to Be Like Jesus discussion. Some of my favorite youth ministry communicators in the world are included on these DVDs. (See page 140.)

In addition to the teaching segments on the DVDs, we've added small group leader tips that are unique to each session. Brett and I give you specific small group pointers and ideas that will help you lead each session. If you spend five to 10 minutes watching the leadership tips and then spend another 10 to 15 minutes reading through each session in advance, you'll be fully equipped to lead students through the material. The DVDs aren't required, but they're a great supplement to the small group material.

In addition, you can find free, helpful tips for leading small groups on our Web site, www.simplyyouthministry.com/lifetogether. These tips are general, so any small group leader may benefit from them. I encourage you to take advantage of these resources!

What STARTING TO GO WHERE GOD WANTS YOU TO BE is all about

Starting to Go Where God Wants You to Be begins with a call to love God and love others, followed by one session on each of the five biblical purposes: fellowship, discipleship, ministry, evangelism, and worship. It's like a table set with great appetizers. You get to taste them all.

I encourage small groups to begin with **Starting to Go Where God Wants You to Be.** Then study the rest of the books in any order—maybe by interest, maybe in an order that prepares you for events on the youth ministry calendar, such as **Sharing Your Story and God's Story** before an evangelism outreach in the fall or **Serving Others in Love** to prepare for the mission trip in the spring. With five other books to choose from, you're in control. There's no "correct" order for using the books.

You're ready to get started!

SURRENDERING

YOUR LIFE TO HONOR GOD

LIVING WORSHIP

Before joining the youth ministry staff at Saddleback Church, my wife Cathy and I visited one of the worship services. I didn't know a lot about the church, but I did know it had a great reputation and was known by pastors all over the world. With this in the back of my mind, I found it comical when I looked through the worship bulletin and found spelling errors. I smugly laughed to myself and was eager to share my discovery with Cathy.

As I nudged her I immediately realized she wouldn't be interested. I could tell by the look in her eyes. She had entered into the worship experience and had already shifted her focus from the rush of getting to church on time to the presence of God. Within minutes of our arrival, she had left the world behind. She was worshiping with passion and thankfulness as I had seen her do thousands of times before.

I, on the other hand, was focusing on the human efforts that went into the bulletin. I had missed the point of being at church, and I was missing out on a great opportunity to worship God.

Cathy was a worshiper. I was a spectator.

When people are asked about worship, many people mention their favorite church songs. Unfortunately in many churches singing and worship are considered the same. But worship is so much more than singing. That's only one component of worship. At its core, worship is surrendering your entire life to God, to his way and his control.

My prayer is that these six sessions will lead you to a more intimate relationship with God. Consider making that your prayer too. You'll never be the same again. Neither will the others in your small group.

FELLOWSHIP: CONNECTING Your Heart to Others'

[goal: to have students share about their lives and listen attentively to others]

To worship we need to take our eyes off ourselves so we can focus on God. When we go too long without worshiping God, the overwhelming details of life begin to weigh us down and ultimately to trap us. That's when we begin to believe we're too busy or too tired to focus on God. So slow down! You don't have to rush through these questions. Use them as a guide to trigger conversation with friends who you want to know better. Relax. Talk. Enjoy.

Brainstorm a list of ways to worship God. Write your ideas down. (If you're stuck, look at page 30 for ideas.)

Write a definition of worship below and then share your definition with the group. (Don't worry about getting it perfect. You'll have a chance to revise it after you've finished this book.)

If you haven't discussed the **Small Group Covenant** on page 88, take time to read it together and discuss it now. Make commitments to one another that your group time will reflect those values. You may want to have one person read the covenant to the group before you begin each lesson as a reminder.

Use the **Small Group Roster** (page 90) to record the names and contact information of the small group members.

DISCIPLESHIP: GROWING to Be Like Jesus

[goal: to explore God's Word, learn biblical knowledge, and make personal applications]

Christians talk a lot about worship, yet somehow misconceptions continue. A lot of the discussions are about the particular styles people prefer. For example, some might talk about their love for contemporary music while others think hymns lead to "real worship." Others prefer silence followed by loud praise songs. Everyone has a preference or two. That's one of the great things about how God has created humanity—we're all different!

But the words to a song, the style of the music, and the environment where Christians gather aren't as important as the heart of the worshiper. The apostle Paul describes worship like this:

> ¹Therefore, I urge you, brothers, in view of God's mercy, to offer your bodies as living sacrifices, holy and pleasing to God—this is your spiritual act of worship. ²Do not conform any longer to the pattern of this world, but be transformed by the renewing of your mind. Then you will be able to test and approve what God's will is—his good, pleasing and perfect will.
>
> ³For by the grace given me I say to every one of you: Do not think of yourself more highly than you ought, but rather think of yourself with sober judgment, in accordance with the measure of faith God has given you.
>
> —Romans 12:1-3

Terms that look like this are described in Learn a Little More near the end of the session.

What personal mercies have you experienced from God? Get specific.

What does it mean to offer your body
as a spiritual act of worship?

What's the relationship between mental transformation ("be transformed by the renewing of your mind") and worship?

What are some signs that you're being
transformed by the renewing of your mind?

Worshiping God leads to renewal, which leads to
transformation. According to this passage, what
follows transformation?

Would you consider yourself to be a discerning
person (meaning that you regularly know the will
of God)? Explain why you think so.

10 How do thoughts about yourself impact your thinking about God?

11 How would you describe the last week or two of your life if you were to look at it through a lens of "sober judgment?"

12 We don't worship God on our own initiative. Worship of God is in response to something. What are we responding to? What specific clues do you find in the text to support your answer?

13 How can a better understanding of God's mercy improve your worship of him?

14 What's the connection between the worship of the heart and the worship that happens within a church building?

MINISTRY: SERVING Others in Love

[goal: to recognize and take opportunities to serve others]

Although you receive spiritual benefit when you worship God, worship is not about you. Worship is about God and honoring him. When you serve others with a right heart, you're also worshiping God with your life.

Below are four actions that will affect your attitude when you serve others. These same actions are also evident when you take time to focus on God and worship him. Next to each attitude evaluate yourself in your worship and in your service. Write a plus (+) if this attitude is a strength of yours and a minus (−) if you need to improve.

Actions	When I worship	When I serve
Appreciation (thankfulness)		
Affirmation (praise, statements of worth)		
Adoration (declarations of love)		
Awareness (a focus on God and his activities)		

Share a few of your answers (perhaps your strongest and weakest areas) and explain why you graded yourself the way you did.

EVANGELISM: SHARING Your Story and God's Story

[goal: to consider how the truths from this lesson might be applied to relationships with unbelievers]

Do you think the following sentence is true or false?

Unbelievers can't worship God since worship flows from a relationship with him. Unbelievers can be ministered to by observing authentic worship in the life of a believer.

 Explain your response. What do you like about this statement? What don't you like?

At the beginning of small groups such as this one, you should decide whether your group is open to inviting friends to join. If your group is open, list who you would like to invite and make plans for talking with them. Your small group leader or your leadership team may have already determined the group is closed at this time. If so, a good group respects and follows that decision. You may be able to invite friends to join you in the next LIFETOGETHER book.

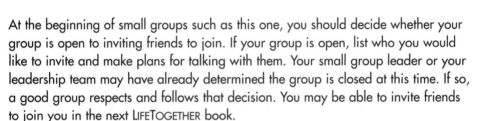

Read **How to Keep Your Small Group from Becoming a Clique** (page 92) when you're at home.

WORSHIP: SURRENDERING Your Life to Honor God

[goal: to focus on God's presence]

Just like breathing, worship can happen naturally in your life. The life-altering difference between breathing and worship is that we don't have to remind ourselves to breathe. It happens naturally. Worship isn't as natural as breathing, so we can find ourselves spiritually suffocating if we're not taking regular opportunities to focus on God.

Worship can be a spiritual form of breathing. At the end of every small group time, you'll be asked to take some spiritual breaths by focusing on God. As you continue to meet together, this will become easier and more natural.

18 End your group time by sharing one goal you have for yourself spiritually. (Choose a goal you can pursue through all six sessions). What do you hope to gain by going through a Bible study on worship?

19 Share one specific way the others in the group can pray for you. Write down the prayer requests. (See the **Prayer Request Log** on page 132.)

20 Pray together as a small group and commit to ending all your small group times with worship.

21 Before your group breaks, read **At Home This Week** together. (If everyone in the group has already done this in another LIFETOGETHER book, you can skip the introduction if you'd like.)

You'll find three prayer resources in the back of the book. By reading and discussing them, you'll find your group prayer time more rewarding.
- 📖 Praying in Your Small Group (page 126). Read this article on your own before the next session.
- 📖 Prayer Request Guidelines (page 128). Read and discuss these guidelines as a group.
- 📖 Prayer Options (page 130). Refer to this list for ideas to give your prayer time variety.

AT HOME THIS WEEK

Each week, you'll have at least four options to help you grow and learn on your own—which means you'll have more to contribute when you return to the group.

Daily Bible Readings
On page 104 you'll find **Daily Bible Readings,** a chart of Bible passages that correspond with the lessons—five for each week. If you choose this option, read one passage each day. Highlight it in your Bible, reflect on it, journal about it, or repeat it

out loud as a prayer. You're free to interact with the Bible verses any way you want, just be sure to read God's love letter—the Bible. You'll find helpful tips in **How to Study the Bible** (page 105).

Memory Verses

Memorizing Bible verses is an important habit to develop as you learn to grow spiritually on your own. **Memory Verses** (page 108) lists six verses—one per week—for you to memorize if you want to plant God's Word in your heart. Memorizing verses (and making them stick for more than a few minutes) isn't easy, but the benefits are undeniable. You'll have God's Word with you wherever you go.

Journaling

You'll find blank pages for journaling beginning on page 113. At the end of each lesson, you'll find several options and a question or two to get your thoughts going—but you aren't limited to the ideas in this book. Use these pages to reflect, to write a letter to God, to note what you're learning, to compose a prayer, to ask a question, to draw a picture of your praise, to record your thoughts. For more suggestions about journaling, turn to **Journaling: Snapshots of Your Heart** (page 110).

If you'd like to choose journaling this week, respond to these questions:

When have you had a great worship experience?
What made it great?

Wrap It Up

Write out your answers to the session questions your group didn't have time to discuss.

This week share with the others in your group which option seems most appealing to try during the coming week. The variety of preferences is another reminder of how different the people in your group are.

During other weeks, take time to share with the group what you did **At Home This Week.**

LEARN A LITTLE MORE

Living sacrifices

Within the context of Old Testament worship, sacrifices (often animals) were offered to God and put to death. The worshiper surrendered something valuable as the sacrifice. When Jesus died on the cross, he became the perfect sacrifice. Since we don't have a need to offer animal sacrifices to cover our sins, our response is to worship

God in thanksgiving and praise and to offer all that we have left—the sacrifice of our living selves.

The sacrifice that we offer to God is described with three ideas:

- Living
- Being Holy (set apart for God)
- Pleasing God

Spiritual act of worship

Our spiritual act of worship is a part of an interesting progression described in this passage:

- God's mercy leads to our worship of him.
- Our worship leads to being renewed by God's presence.
- Our renewal leads to our minds being transformed.
- Our mental transformation leads to the ability to know God's will.
- In this context, we ought to consider ourselves with sober judgment (or as the New Living Translation puts it, be honest in your estimate of yourselves).

Here are a few specific ways to worship:

- Praying (Psalm 95:6)
- Hearing the Word (John 17:17; Deuteronomy 31:11)
- Giving (1 Corinthians 16:1-2)
- Baptizing (Romans 6:3-4)
- Meditating and being silent (Habakkuk 2:20)
- Celebrating the Lord's Supper (1 Corinthians 11:23-26)
- Singing (Ephesians 5:19)
- Celebrating the arts (Exodus 35:30-36:7)

Transformed

This word means to be changed from one form to another, often a major change. God wants to change us. He wants us to be like Jesus, not the world. Transformation happens when we allow God's Word and his Spirit to renew our minds and clear our vision so we can walk God's way.

FOR FURTHER STUDY

Revelation 15:4
Psalm 2:11
Joshua 24:14-18

NOTES

If you are watching the LifeTogether DVD, you may use this page to take notes.

NOTES

WORTHY OF WORSHIP

Have you ever had one of those days that you thought was going to be great but turned out to be one of the worst days of your life? I'm sure everyone has...at least once.

One that's high on my list happened on a Monday. I had just returned from the youth group winter retreat. We had a great weekend! Many students returned home with changed lives and a passion to follow God's ways. I was thrilled. I couldn't wait to get to the church office on Monday morning and tell everyone about the results. Actually, in the back of my mind, I assumed they had already heard about the weekend and were going to tell me how wonderful I was for leading such an impactful camp. I fully expected to be praised for a job well done.

When I arrived at the church. I was immediately reprimanded because the church vans were messy and parked in the wrong place. My boss yelled at me because the church megaphone had been broken at the retreat. Everyone in the office seemed mad at me for something.

I couldn't take any more after a few minutes. I left feeling angry, misunderstood, betrayed, and worthless. I wanted to quit *that day* and let them look for another youth minister who would love the students as much as I did. I was depressed. I was a pitiful sight.

My biggest surprise came soon after. In my spiritually weakened condition, when I felt very small, I had a moment when God seemed really big. He spoke to me, not in an audible voice, but with impact in my spirit. He reminded me that I don't live and work for the applause of humans. I have been created to serve him, so as long as I keep my eyes focused on him, I'll have the power I need to continue—even when days don't go my way. He reminded me of his power and purposes for my life.

My tears of pain became tears of joy. When I was reminded of how big and powerful God is, all I wanted to do was praise him. Worship him. Really. That's all I could do. When you realize how big God is, only one response is adequate: worship.

Learn together of God's goodness and power. He's worthy of your worship.

FELLOWSHIP: CONNECTING Your Heart to Others'

Talk about this question:

If you had all of God's power, what would you do with it?

DISCIPLESHIP: GROWING to Be Like Jesus

The book of Psalms is unique because it's both God's Word to believers *and* the believers' words back to him. You can read the Psalms as God's word to you and learn about him and his ways. And you can pray the Psalms back to God, you can pray and worship him the way he intends. The more you read and learn about God's character, the more you'll find that he's easy to worship. Trusting him with your entire life... that's more difficult, but even that becomes easier as your understanding of his true nature increases.

¹I will exalt you, my God the King;
    I will praise your name for ever and ever.
²Every day I will praise you
    and extol your name for ever and ever.
³Great is the Lord and most worthy of praise;
    his greatness no one can fathom.
⁴One generation will commend your works to another;
    they will tell of your mighty acts.
⁵They will speak of the glorious splendor of your majesty,
    and I will meditate on your wonderful works.
⁶They will tell of the power of your awesome works,
    and I will proclaim your great deeds.
⁷They will celebrate your abundant goodness
    and joyfully sing of your righteousness.
⁸The Lord is gracious and compassionate,

SURRENDERING your life to honor God

slow to anger and rich in love.
⁹The Lord is good to all;
   he has compassion on all he has made.
¹⁰All you have made will praise you, O Lord;
   your saints will extol you.
¹¹They will tell of the glory of your kingdom
   and speak of your might,
¹²so that all men may know of your mighty acts
   and the glorious splendor of your kingdom.
¹³Your kingdom is an everlasting kingdom,
   and your dominion endures through all generations.
The Lord is faithful to all his promises
   and loving toward all he has made.
¹⁴The Lord upholds all those who fall
   and lifts up all who are bowed down.
¹⁵The eyes of all look to you,
   and you give them their food at the proper time.
¹⁶You open your hand
   and satisfy the desires of every living thing.
¹⁷The Lord is righteous in all his ways
   and loving toward all he has made.
¹⁸The Lord is near to all who call on him,
   to all who call on him in truth.
¹⁹He fulfills the desires of those who fear him;
   he hears their cry and saves them.
²⁰The Lord watches over all who love him,
   but all the wicked he will destroy.
²¹My mouth will speak in praise of the Lord.
   Let every creature praise his holy name
   for ever and ever.

—Psalm 145

As you reread this Psalm underline all the reasons the psalmist praises God.

   Circle the phrases that stand out to you as most significant. Explain why they make an impression.

Verse 5 reads, "I will meditate on your wonderful works." What does it mean to meditate?

- ⌨ Describe what a person meditating on Scripture might do.
- ⌨ Have you ever done this before?
- ⌨ Why would meditating on the Word help you grow spiritually?

3

Look back at verse 8 to see a common description of God. In your own words, what does it mean?

- ⌨ What events or stories in the Bible do you know that reinforce the truth about God's character in this verse?

4

5 Verse 13 reads, "The Lord is faithful to all his promises." What God-fulfilled promises have you experienced in your life? Be as specific and personal as possible.

6 Verses 14–20 describe specific things God does. Look through these verses again. Which one seems most important to you—for you?

Skim through Psalm 145 and point out clues that describe the kind of attitudes you ought to have toward God.

7

SURRENDERING your life to honor God

MINISTRY: SERVING Others in Love

After I returned from the retreat and had my meltdown, my view of ministry changed. My motivation changed from pleasing others to serving God. When I began to live for God's approval instead of the approval of others, my ministry and my life went in a whole new direction. Without a reminder of the power of God, I probably would have quit out of frustration.

8 What is one area of your life where you feel powerless (relationships, ego, reputation, approval...)? How does it affect your desire, ability, or opportunity to serve God?

9 If you had direct access to God's power, would it make a difference in how you live? How could God's power improve your ability to serve him?

10 2 Corinthians 13:4 says, "Although [Jesus] died on the cross in weakness, he now lives by the mighty power of God. We, too, are weak, but we live in him and have God's power—the power we use in dealing with you" (**NLT**). Based on this verse, we **do** have access to God's power. How do you get it from the Spirit into your life?

11 Turn to the **Spiritual Health Assessment** (on page 37). Take a few minutes to rate yourself in the **SURRENDER Your Life to Honor God** section. (You don't have to share your scores with the group.)

If you've never taken the Spiritual Health Assessment, consider taking the time to complete the remaining four areas later this week.

EVANGELISM: SHARING Your Story and God's Story

Most people who come to Jesus see something attractive in the life of a believer that moves them along in their own spiritual journey.

Read this scenario together.

A new brother and sister arrive at your school. They're both attractive and seem genuinely friendly. As you get to know them, you discover they're totally committed to living God's way. It's obvious that they honor God with their lifestyles. They aren't weird or religious, but you realize they believe God is who he says he is. They live their lives with faith and trust God's promises and his power.

🔲 How will unbelievers respond to this brother and sister?

🔲 How will Christians respond to them?

What makes a believer's life attractive to an unbeliever?

 # WORSHIP: SURRENDERING Your Life to Honor God

Break into pairs. With your partner, finish this sentence: "I believe God is worth worshiping because..."

For the rest of the weeks your group is working through this book, let this person be your spiritual partner. Whenever your group breaks into pairs again, get together with your spiritual partner.

It's a normal part of group life to have a closer connection with some people than with others. If you find this to be the case and you'd like to spend more time throughout the week talking about life and challenging one another spiritually, consider using the **Accountability Questions** on page 94.

Share prayer requests with your entire group. Be sure to write them down on the **Prayer Request Log** (page 132) so you can look back to see how God answers your prayers. Spend time praying together:

- **In praise:** Thank God for his greatness and power.

- **In silence:** Listen for God's promptings, his impressions, his voice.

- **In request:** Pray to personally understand God's greatness better so that your natural response will be to worship him with your life. Then pray for the requests of your group members.

AT HOME THIS WEEK

Daily Bible Readings
Check out the Scriptures on page 104.

Memory Verses
Try memorizing a verse from page 108.

Journaling
Use **SCRIBBLE** pages, 113-125
- Write whatever is on your mind.
- Read your journal entry from last week and write a reflection on it.
- Respond to this question: *What do I need to better understand God's power?*

Wrap It Up
Write out your answers to the session questions your group didn't have time to discuss.

LEARN A LITTLE MORE

Exalt
To raise high, lift up to a worthy position.

King
In our era of democracy, kings are out of fashion. We don't trust people who claim the right to rule, because we've seen power abused so often. The authors of the U.S. Constitution mistrusted kings so much that they created a government in which no leader could have too much power.

Someone in the universe *has* the right to be called King. He has the right to rule, not because he has been elected by his citizens, but because he made his citizens and he is a thoroughly trustworthy ruler. Absolute power will not corrupt him. Does God deserve to be our King? This question addresses a central issue for us.

Extol
To praise highly, glorify.

Gracious and compassionate...slow to anger
The Bible describes God as "gracious and compassionate" and "slow to anger" nine times. Grace is a fundamental part of God's character. Sadly, some Christians feel as though God is always angry with them and harshly judging them like a dictator—and they tend to transfer the anger and judgment to other people.

The truth about God and grace is important for evangelism. God's grace is central to the message of the gospel. God will judge the world (look back at Psalm 145:20), but it takes *so much* to get him angry (he's slow to anger), and he's quick to show compassion to anyone who calls out to him.

> ### Gracious and compassionate
> Exodus 34:6; 2 Chronicles 30:9; Nehemiah 9:17; Psalm 86:15; 103:8; 111:4; 145:8; Joel 2:13; Jonah 4:2
> ### Slow to anger
> Exodus 34:6; Numbers 14:18; Nehemiah 9:17; Psalm 86:15; 103:8; 145:8; Joel 2:13; Jonah 4:2; Nahum 1:3.

FOR FURTHER STUDY

Isaiah 40:28-31; 44:6-8
1 Chronicles 29:11-12

NOTES

NOTES

SURRENDERING YOUR PAST

If you've already studied the LIFETOGETHER book **Growing to Be Like Jesus**, you'll remember Brett and Dee Eastman. When they found out they were having triplets, they were thrilled. The months leading up to the birth were all about dreams, decorating, and investigating what life with triplets would be like. They were having fun imagining how three more children would impact their lives.

Unfortunately, events changed dramatically and quickly. The fun was over. In the 28th week Dee prematurely gave birth to Melody without a doctor's help. Dee needed an emergency C-section to deliver the other two babies, but they had to wait 30 minutes for the doctor to arrive and perform the operation. During the delay several things went wrong, and as a result Meagan and Michelle have cerebral palsy. Meagan may never walk or talk, and Michelle is affected to a lesser degree.

Imagine the pain Brett and Dee felt. Bitterness about the doctor's late arrival lasted every day for several years. It wasn't until Brett and Dee joined a small group that they begin to make peace with the past. As they discussed what it meant to worship God with their entire lives, the bitterness issue kept coming up. They knew that, in order to keep growing spiritually, they needed to give the situation to God. They needed to surrender everything—their hurt, their sorrows, and their daughters' lives.

Surrender moved them toward forgiveness and healing. After many months of prayer and talking with their small group friends, they made an appointment to see the doctor. They wanted to forgive him face to face. The meeting was full of tears, but also forgiveness and love. Dee and Brett have never been the same. When they surrendered their past to God, their present took on a new meaning.

What's in your past that you're hanging on to? It may not be as life-changing as the Eastmans' experience—or it may be even more impactful. Surrendering pain from the past isn't easy, but it's a vital step to keep you moving forward and growing in your relationship with God. To worship with your life is to surrender everything and ask God to take your emptied self and fill you with himself.

This might be a painful session, but that's why you're in a small group. You don't have to go through pain alone. Surrender your past and look forward to God's work in your future.

FELLOWSHIP: CONNECTING Your Heart to Others'

Describe an event you remember that has helped shape you today.

DISCIPLESHIP: GROWING to Be Like Jesus

You can't change your past whether it's positive or painful. Your painful past has the potential to haunt you and paralyze your future choices. Many Christians allow themselves to become prisoners or victims of their past. If you choose that path, it leads nowhere and keeps you from becoming the person God created you to become.

The Bible helps us see that no past is so painful or prideful that God can't heal it and no past is so sinful that God won't forgive it.

As you'll see in this section, a past doesn't have to be horrific for it to be surrendered. You'll see how the apostle Paul refused to allow his elite past to control his future. He called it trash when compared to knowing Jesus.

Worshiping God requires you to surrender your past—both painful and successful—so you can clearly focus on the One who controls your future.

If anyone else thinks he has reasons to put confidence in the flesh, I have more: ⁵circumcised on the eighth day, of the people of Israel, of the tribe of Benjamin, a Hebrew of Hebrews; in regard to the law, a Pharisee; ⁶as for zeal, persecuting the church; as for legalistic righteousness, faultless.
⁷But whatever was to my profit I now consider loss for the sake of Christ. ⁸What is more, I consider everything a loss compared to the surpassing greatness of knowing Christ Jesus my Lord, for whose sake I have lost all things. I consider them rubbish, that I may gain Christ ⁹and be found in him, not having a righteousness of my own that

comes from the law, but that which is through faith in Christ—the righteousness that comes from God and is by faith. [10]I want to know Christ and the power of his resurrection and the fellowship of sharing in his sufferings, becoming like him in his death, [11]and so, somehow, to attain to the resurrection from the dead.

—Philippians 3:4-11

Based on this passage and other Bible passages you may know, what do you know of Paul's character?

Paul considered his past as a loss for the sake of Christ (verse 7). What things from your past may be keeping you from knowing Jesus and living for him to the fullest?

What are some positives from your past that may have a negative impact on your faith today?

What's the difference between righteousness from the law and righteousness from faith (verse 9)?

Paul makes it clear that all believers have access to the power of God—the same power that raised Jesus from the dead. Do you regularly rely on God's power?

🔲 In practical terms, how can you know when you're relying on God's power?

What did Paul want from God that made him willing to surrender his past?

Paul's negative past included persecuting Christians (verse 6), even helping kill them. How would you go about surrendering such a big-time sin to God?

🔲 How should so-called lesser sins be surrendered to God?

MINISTRY: SERVING Others in Love

Many people who live on the streets in my community are plagued by their pasts. As I've spoken with them, I find that they made some terrible decisions and the consequences have led them to the streets. Their past squashes their hope for the future. It not only haunts them, but it molds who they are today. Homeless people are everywhere.

9 In Matthew 25:40 Jesus said, "I assure you, when you [cared for] one of the least of these my brothers and sisters, you were doing it to me!" What did Jesus mean by this statement?

What might your small group do to minister to the homeless who are plagued by their past? First consider where you might find them. Then put together an action plan for your small group to serve these people. Take care to treat them with dignity.

EVANGELISM: SHARING Your Story and God's Story

Give one word to describe what your past was like before you surrendered it to follow God's way.

11

What difference has God made in your life?

12

Jesus' life, death, and resurrection is the greatest story ever told. That's God's story. Your answers to the first two questions in this section combine to create the second greatest story ever told—your testimony. Your story describes how God has impacted your life. If you've never written down your story, turn to **My Story** (page 87). Work on it this week when you're at home.

Have you shared your story with others? If you have, what has the response of your listeners been? If not, ask God for an opportunity to share it with someone in the near future.

13

WORSHIP: SURRENDERING Your Life to Honor God

Read the following three Bible verses:

Then I said, "My destruction is sealed, for I am a sinful man and a member of a sinful race. Yet I have seen the King, the Lord Almighty!"

—Isaiah 6:5 NLT

I will go home to my father and say, "Father, I have sinned against both heaven and you, and I am no longer worthy of being called your son. Please take me on as a hired man."

—Luke 15:18-19 NLT

I will call on the Lord, who is worthy of praise, for he saves me from my enemies.

—Psalm 18:3 NLT

Draw a line from each term to the corresponding verse.

Surrender of fear
Surrender of disobedience
Surrender of bad decisions

Which of these "surrenders" is the one you want to pay closer attention to in your life?

Close the group time by praying together. If you haven't already, consider surrendering your past to God. Ask him to take it from you, forgive you, cleanse you, and help you honor him with your life.

Dealing with pain from your past can be big. You need courage, faith, and help to deal with the feelings and memories that usually accompany it. Be sure to talk with someone—a parent, a youth leader, a trusted teen or adult friend, a pastor—about it. Burying it only makes it worse. If you're not ready to talk right now, don't wait too long to face it.

AT HOME THIS WEEK

Daily Bible Readings
Check out the Scriptures on page 104.

Memory Verses
Try memorizing a verse from page 108.

Journaling
Use **SCRIBBLE** pages, 113-125
- Write whatever is on your mind.
- Read your journal entry from last week and write a reflection on it.
- Respond to these questions:
  What is the most painful experience of my past?
  How has it impacted me?
  Have I surrendered it to God and asked him to free me of it?
  If not, what is keeping me from surrender?

Wrap It Up
Write out your answers to the session questions your group didn't have time to discuss.

LEARN A LITTLE MORE

Circumcised...of Israel...of Benjamin...a Hebrew of Hebrews...a Pharisee...zeal[ous]...faultless
All of these terms describe the ideal Jew. Circumcision was the mark of a Jewish male. Paul belonged to the Pharisees, the most respected men within Judaism because of their supposed piety. He could even claim to have followed all the rules of the religion. Paul was saying that he had done everything to be respected in the eyes of the world.

Persecuting the church
Paul helped to lead the earliest efforts to stamp out the followers of Jesus. Acts 7:54-8:3 describes his participation in the murder of Stephen. Acts 9 tells how God revealed himself to Paul while Paul was in the middle of his anti-Christian crusade.

Righteousness of my own that comes from the law

If you were to total all the laws in the Old Testament, they'd add up to 612. God gave the Ten Commandments (and the other 602 laws) to Moses so that the Israelites would know how to live the good life he wants for his people. The Law defined perfection. That's all the Law can do, really—define perfection. Because no one is perfect, the Law shows how imperfect we are. The Law can't help us be perfect. Once you're firmly convinced that you can't be perfect, you're in a position to place your faith fully in Jesus and receive his free gift of salvation.

And so, somehow, to attain to the resurrection from the dead

Paul's statement doesn't mean that he questioned his status as a believer, as if he were unsure that God will keep his promises. The uncertainty in this passage isn't about whether he'd spend eternity in heaven but how it would come about. Paul was convinced the resurrection would happen; he just didn't know how.

I know that tomorrow the sun will rise. I don't understand everything that's involved with it. I've been told the sun stands still and the earth rotates on its own axis, but that information isn't helpful. I don't understand gravity, though I know it's an invisible force that keeps us moving around the sun. What's that about? Why doesn't gravity take a day off? Doesn't it ever get tired? Why don't we spin faster some days and slower on others? If a rock lands on our planet from outer space, does that get us off track a little? Although I have tons of (meaningless) questions about the sun rising tomorrow, I know beyond a shadow of a doubt (pun intended) that it will happen.

FOR FURTHER STUDY

John 17:3
1 John 2:3-4, 13; 5:20

NOTES

SURRENDERING YOUR FUTURE

By the time you reach high school, it becomes apparent that life isn't filled with everything you had hoped for. As a child you may have been protected and taken care of, but as a teenager you begin to feel the painful consequences of your decisions. In the midst of navigating your current life, you develop thoughts, dreams, and hopes regarding your future. It's good to think about your future, and it's important that you have hope where your future is concerned. It's terrible to be hopeless.

Hope is future-oriented; it's wanting and believing in something you don't have. In between the present and the future is a wait. While you're waiting, you have choices about your attitude.

One option is to wait with an attitude of despair. Either the pain from the past or troubled feelings of the present causes despair. The problem with despair is that it kills hope. Despair is one option, but not a great one.

Fear is another attitude that looms between the present and the future. A lot of people are consumed with fear because they can't control, anticipate, or predict their futures. It's a popular choice. When you investigate fear, you'll usually find it's fueled by a lack of confidence in God's plan and faithfulness.

Another attitude—far superior to despair and fear—is faith. Faith keeps you focused on God's trustworthiness. Faith doesn't run away when you feel bad or when you don't get what you want.

The greatest growth in my spiritual life came when I finally understood that I needed to give my future to God and trust him to be in control. Until I did, I couldn't get rid of despair and fear. They kept showing up and derailing my growth. Giving God my future was the ultimate act of surrender for me. I surrendered my past and received forgiveness, I surrendered my present and received guidance, and I finally surrendered my future and received peace. Peace came when I had faith that God cares more about my future than I do.

Now I can worship God with my life because I'm not worried. I can either live my life for worship or for worry. I chose worship, and God hasn't let me down. My life isn't perfect, but during the difficult times I live by faith that God is who he says he is and that he'll do what he's promised to do. Since I can't control my future, I entrust it to God.

In this session, you'll be challenged to take what you don't know about your future and place it in the hands of the One who knows your future and cares more about it than you do. Encourage one another, because this isn't an easy step to take.

FELLOWSHIP: CONNECTING Your Heart to Others'

1 Describe what you hope your life will be like when you're 30 years old.

2 How might your relationship with God be impacted if your life doesn't end up like you hope it will?

DISCIPLESHIP: GROWING to Be Like Jesus

Surrendering your future requires you to trust in God's character and his promises even when you don't know the outcome of your life. You're saying, "God, I don't know my future, but I don't want to take my focus off you to worry about it. I want to worship you. I place my faith in your character, and I will trust the promises from your Word. I surrender to your goodness."

As you read this passage from Hebrews, take notice that these heroes of faith responded to God's promises. They surrendered their futures to God and now they have the title *people of faith*.

¹Now faith is being sure of what we hope for and certain of what we do not see. ²This is what the ancients were commended for.

³By faith we understand that the universe was formed at God's command, so that what is seen was not made out of what was visible...

⁶And without faith it is impossible to please God, because anyone who comes to him must believe that he

SURRENDERING your life to honor God

exists and that he rewards those who earnestly seek him.

⁷By faith Noah, when warned about things not yet seen, in holy fear built an ark to save his family. By his faith he condemned the world and became heir of the righteousness that comes by faith.

⁸By faith Abraham, when called to go to a place he would later receive as his inheritance, obeyed and went, even though he did not know where he was going. ⁹By faith he made his home in the promised land like a stranger in a foreign country; he lived in tents, as did Isaac and Jacob, who were heirs with him of the same promise. ¹⁰For he was looking forward to the city with foundations, whose architect and builder is God.

¹¹By faith Abraham, even though he was past age— and Sarah herself was barren—was enabled to become a father because he considered him faithful who had made the promise. ¹²And so from this one man, and he as good as dead, came descendants as numerous as the stars in the sky and as countless as the sand on the seashore.

¹³All these people were still living by faith when they died. They did not receive the things promised; they only saw them and welcomed them from a distance. And they admitted that they were aliens and strangers on earth. ¹⁴People who say such things show that they are looking for a country of their own. ¹⁵If they had been thinking of the country they had left, they would have had opportunity to return. ¹⁶Instead, they were longing for a better country—a heavenly one. Therefore God is not ashamed to be called their God, for he has prepared a city for them.

—Hebrews 11:1-3, 6-16

3 Look back at verses 1 and 6. What are the core components of faith as described in these verses?

4 What are the things you hope for as a Christian and do not yet see?

5 Why do you think it's impossible to please God without faith?
- Does this statement seem harsh or unfair?
- How would you explain this truth to an unbeliever?

6 Why is believing that God rewards those who seek him an important part of faith?

7 This passage highlights some ancient heroes of faith. Who in your life do you respect because of their faith and devotion?

8 What similarities do you see between the faiths of Noah and Abraham?

9 Reread verse 3 and respond to the following statement:
Since we believe God created the universe, we have no reason to study evolution.
- What do you like about this statement?
- What don't you like?

Reread verses 13–16. How can the promise of a "better country, a heavenly one" impact the way you live today?

10

11
When you consider the condition of your life, do you think God is ashamed to be identified with you? Why do you think that?

12
Describe the last time you didn't get something you hoped for. How did you feel? Did God let you down? Were you hoping for the wrong thing?
💻 If we know God never lets us down, why do we sometimes still feel as though he has?

MINISTRY: SERVING Others in Love

Many Christians understand that they're called to serve God by serving others, but a lot of people want to serve God on their own terms.

What do you think about this statement?
I want to serve God as long as he doesn't want me to work in the AIDS-infested regions of Africa.

13

Can you be fully surrendered to God's will and still express desires about what you do and don't want?

What does God think about your desires and feelings?

Discuss how your thoughts about your future and the act of surrender might collide.

EVANGELISM: SHARING Your Story and God's Story

A common fear Christians have is they will be rejected if they share their own story along with God's story. It's rooted in fear of the unknown or fear of the future. When you surrender your future to God, you're trusting God with your evangelistic efforts too.

"Such love has no fear because perfect love expels all fear. If we are afraid, it is for fear of judgment, and this shows that his love has not been perfected in us" (1 John 4:18 **NLT**). How might the truth of this verse impact your evangelistic actions and attitude?

18 Can you be a person of faith and have still have fear about some actions (such as sharing your story)?

19 My Story—As you surrender your entire life to God (past, present, and future), God can and will use you to point others toward him. It can be scary, but your faith will grow as you trust God. Write down names of a few family members, friends, or acquaintances you know who would benefit from you sharing your story and God's story with them. Next to each name, write out an action plan for sharing with that person.

Name	Plan

WORSHIP: SURRENDERING Your Life to Honor God

Below are some areas of your future to surrender to God. Check off the ones that you have the most difficulty giving over to God at this point in your life.

◇ My friendships

◇ My purity

◇ My job

◇ My sports

◇ My time

◇ My boyfriend

◇ My girlfriend

◇ My family

◇ My addictions

◇ My ministry

◇ My dreams

◇ My goals

◇ My popularity

◇ My _____

◇ My _____

◇ My _____

◇ My _____

◇ My _____

◇ My _____

Team up with your spiritual partner (or someone else if necessary) and share which of the following attitudes describes what you feel about your future.

Despair
Fear
Faith

Pray for one another that God will give you whatever you need to trust him with your future while living for him in the present.

AT HOME THIS WEEK

Daily Bible Readings
Check out the Scriptures on page 104.

Memory Verses
Try memorizing a verse from page 108.

Journaling
Use **SCRIBBLE** pages, 113-125
- Write whatever is on your mind.
- Read your journal entry from last week and write a reflection on it.
- Respond to this question: *If you could do anything for God with your life and you knew you wouldn't fail, what would you like to do?*

Wrap It Up
Write out your answers to the session questions your group didn't have time to discuss.

LEARN A LITTLE MORE

Faith
This classic chapter defines faith, tells us what to put faith in, and inspires us with great examples.

Faith is a sense of certainty and confidence that something promised will happen in the future. Faith has the eye on the future so we know we have firm footing today.

Many critics of the Bible and Christianity don't like the "exclusivity" taught in the Bible. They think it's unfair that faith in the biblical Jesus is absolutely necessary. Telling them that it's impossible to please God without faith only adds fuel to the fire.

As we consider what and how we communicate with unbelievers, we need to include the *entire* story. Faith is essential, but what else? God is *good* and he *rewards* those who seek him.

Selfishness isn't considered an attractive trait—with good reason. Normal selfishness looks out for "me" at the expense of others. Let me challenge you to change your perspective. Regular selfishness means loving yourself, but God loves us far more than we could ever love ourselves. He wants to reward everyone who seeks him. In the end, we'll get more through God's love for us than our love for ourselves.

I'm not suggesting that he rewards us with material blessings; I'm referring to something far better—the condition of your soul. *God loves you!* He loves you more than you can understand. He's shaping you here for something in the world to come (1 Peter 2:5). He knows your potential and will give to everyone who seeks him. No one in his right mind could turn his rewards down.

Noah

Noah lived hundreds of miles from the ocean, but when God instructed him to build a huge ship—Noah responded with faith. Neighbors must have laughed and thought Noah was crazy, yet Noah obeyed because he had surrendered his life to God. (See Genesis 6:1-9:29.)

Abraham...Sarah

At the age of 75, Abraham obeyed God and moved his entire household hundreds of miles to a place where he knew no one. Sarah had to wait decades to receive the baby God promised. Many times we doubt God and question our faith when we don't receive what we want instantly, but God lives by a different timeline than we do. God is all-knowing. Some of his promises are fulfilled in decades and centuries, but he always fulfills them. (See Genesis 12:1-25:11.)

A city

See Revelation 21-22 for a description of the city that awaits us.

FOR FURTHER STUDY

Genesis 5:2; 15:1-6
Matthew 8:5-13; 14:31

NOTES

NOTES

WORSHIPING GOD OR WORSHIPING IDOLS

Prior to moving into our current home we looked at about 50 other houses. After a while, they were all looking the same until we walked into "Psycho House" as my teenage daughter named it. As soon as we walked in the front door, our eyes jumped to the corner of the living room where we saw a shrine displaying idols. I'm not sure what the religious background of the family was nor the meaning of the idols, but there was definitely some funky type of worship happening there. I've been around long enough to realize that idols are not just an Old Testament thing, but I wasn't used to seeing them displayed so prominently in a suburban neighborhood. To be honest, it was creepy.

A simple definition of idol worship is "something or someone who is an object of your affection." An idol doesn't have to be a little ceramic statue. It can be television, instant messaging, a boyfriend or girlfriend, a car, money, friends, a collection of autographed baseball cards...basically anything that you love more than God.

No one wants to admit to worshiping an idol. It sounds so weird—even evil. But we all should evaluate how we spend our time and what has our affections. Other clues are what we spend our money on, what we feel we can't live without, and where we turn when we feel hurt, frustrated, or empty.

Maybe you find it hard to believe, but most Christians worship an idol at some point during their spiritual journeys. You can take a step forward (or a lot of steps) in your spiritual journey when you identify your idols and surrender them to God.

In this session you'll be discussing your idols and ways to keep them from taking God's role in your life. A life focused on worshiping God can have no other idols.

FELLOWSHIP: CONNECTING Your Heart to Others'

From time to time I hear students in our youth ministry say things like, "I could never go a week without TV" or "If I ever lost access to the Web, I can't imagine how prehistoric my life would be." While these might appear like statements of exaggeration, they're spoken with passion and conviction, and they're very convincing. I believe the students most of the time.

What do you love that you can't imagine living without?

1

2 What don't you have that you **really** would like to own? Why is it so important to you?

What's your reaction to this statement:

3

   The answers you gave to the first two questions could potentially take God's place in your life.
   📌 Could this statement be true for you? Explain.

DISCIPLESHIP: GROWING to Be Like Jesus

The Israelites worshiped God but often turned to other gods. During the era of the judges—after the patriarchs, before the kings—the nation of Israel went through cycles of worshiping other gods (among other sins), being conquered by enemies as judgment, repentance, and a return to peace. They were faithful at being inconsistent. If it weren't so sad, their inconsistency would be comical.

At another point in their history, God sent the prophet Jeremiah to confront the Israelites about their unfaithfulness:

> [11]"... Has a nation ever changed its gods?
>   (Yet they are not gods at all.)
> But my people have exchanged their Glory
>   for worthless idols.
> [12]Be appalled at this, O heavens,
>   and shudder with great horror,"
>   declares the Lord.
> [13]"My people have committed two sins:
> They have forsaken me,
>   the spring of living water,
> and have dug their own cisterns,
>   broken cisterns that cannot hold water."
>   —Jeremiah 2:11-13

Of all the names for God, why is he called "their Glory?"
- How is this name significant?
- Why didn't Jeremiah call him something like "the glorious one?"

Why should the heavens shudder with horror when people worship idols?

6 In your own words, explain the two sins in verse 13.

7 Jeremiah says that the Israelites have dug their own cisterns (water tanks)—ones that don't even work right. How is worshiping an idol like digging your own cistern?
■ Describe a time when you tried to take control over an area of your life and it didn't work out right.

8 The first of the 10 commandments says, "I am the Lord your God, who brought you out of Egypt, out of the land of slavery. You shall have no other gods before me" (Exodus 20:2–3). Why can this possibly be so important to God?

9 In Jeremiah's time, every nation had a favorite god or gods they worshiped. Why would the entire nation of Israel give up on God and switch to pieces of wood or stone?

10 Why do we get sidetracked so easily from worshiping God and get caught up serving idols?

11 Let's go personal. What are some ways you've forsaken God? What is something that typically takes priority in place of God? (We've all worshiped idols at some time. No need to pretend otherwise.)

EVANGELISM: SHARING Your Story and God's Story

If idols take over God's rightful place in our lives, then unbelievers have some kind of idol in God's place (because by definition unbelievers don't have God in his rightful place). I don't suggest you accuse them of idol worship, but I do recommend that you consider how this idol image can help you share your story and God's story.

If an idol takes God's place, it also serves as a source of comfort when life gets tough. The good news is that God is the only source of comfort that doesn't eventually lead to disappointment.

Because Christians have to face life struggles just like unbelievers have to, you can share about Jesus by sharing how he helps you with your struggles.

12 What are some difficult experiences you've had that God has helped you through? How did he help you? (Scripture, Christian friends, Bible study...)

What would you say to an unbelieving friend facing your same struggle? **13**
🔲 How can you explain the powerlessness of their idols in a way that they can hear what you are saying?

MINISTRY: SERVING Others in Love

A major reason people will turn to the temporary satisfaction of idols is because they're focusing on themselves and not on others. A self-focus rather than an others-focus is a quick route to idol worship. Serving others is a good way to keep focused on God.

How can your small group serve to keep the idea of ministry fresh within your sights? Are there actions your group can take every week or every day that will help you keep ministry a high priority and outside influences a low priority? List your ideas.

Who will take the lead to make sure these ministry opportunities are fresh each week?

WORSHIP: SURRENDERING Your Life to Honor God

Below is a list of sources people turn to fill their needs. Some of these are embarrassing to admit. Some (such as food) are good things that need to be put in their proper places. Take a moment to scan the list.

What matters more to you than it should?

Is there anything you'd like to share with the group? Now's your chance.

shopping

pornography

the Internet

money

my home life

a relationship

my job

my family

fame

my body

drugs

sports

a hobby

popularity

the television

perfectionism

beauty

acceptance

food

alcohol

ministry

dieting

power

exercise

books

fantasies

compliments

recognition

other _____

other _____

You may not want to share your particular idol with the whole group. Consider talking with one person or an adult leader after the meeting (or at another time). Ask God to give you the strength to rely on him more than your idol.

Have someone read aloud the following Scripture verses. During this time, the other group members can pray silently and offer to God the idol they most struggle with.

17

¹Come, all you who are thirsty,
    come to the waters;
and you who have no money,
    come, buy and eat!
Come, buy wine and milk
    without money and without cost.
²Why spend money on what is not bread,
    and your labor on what does not satisfy?
Listen, listen to me, and eat what is good,

> and your soul will delight in the richest of fare.
> ³Give ear and come to me;
>   hear me, that your soul may live.
> —Isaiah 55:1-3
>
> ¹As the deer pants for streams of water,
>   so my soul pants for you, O God.
> ²My soul thirsts for God, for the living God.
>   When can I go and meet with God?
> —Psalm 42:1-2

Close in prayer. Use the **Prayer Request Log** on page 132.

18

AT HOME THIS WEEK

Daily Bible Readings
Check out the Scriptures on page 104.

Memory Verses
Try memorizing a verse from page 108.

Journaling
Use **SCRIBBLE** pages, 113-125
- Write whatever is on your mind.
- Read your journal entry from last week and write a reflection on it.
- Respond to these questions: *How do I rate my ability to trust God on a scale of 1 (I'm fully dependent on an idol) to 10 (I completely trust God)? Why?*

Wrap It Up
Write out your answers to the session questions your group didn't have time to discuss.

LEARN A LITTLE MORE

Living water
In our age when we can turn on a tap and get all the water we want, we have

a hard time relating to the idea that our lives are dependent on water. People rarely die of thirst.

Originally this expression simply meant running water (as opposed to a still lake). In the Middle East, with a near-desert climate, every drop of water was precious. In fact, gods of rain and rivers were among the most popular gods during Jeremiah's day. People were willing to worship whomever they thought provided the water they needed to survive.

The Lord is the true source of water—for the body and the soul.

Broken cisterns

Without water the people who wandered the desert would die within days. A cistern was their lifeline. As the rains flowed down the mountainside, it was trapped in a holding tank made of rocks and clay. A leaky cistern put lives at risk. It would have been a disaster to think a cistern was full of water only to find out the water had leaked out. What a vivid word picture of getting our needs met apart from God!

FOR FURTHER STUDY

Isaiah 42:17; 57:10-13
John 4:4-15, 7:37-39
1 Corinthians 6:12
2 Peter 2:19

NOTES

If you are watching the LifeTogether DVD, you may use this page to take notes.

NO REGRETS

For a fun, cheap, and creative date, take a picnic lunch and some lounge chairs and head to a local Little League field. Find a place on the sidelines and watch the baseball games of the youngest children. The players are amusing as they dance in the outfield, chase butterflies, run to the wrong bases...the fun never ends. It's better than a movie.

One of the unique elements of this experience is watching parents. From the objective standpoint of the sidelines, you'll see adults who place too much value on things that don't matter. Some are more concerned about winning than their six-year-old flower-pickers. Some shout angrily at their children for missing the ball. A few scream at the volunteer umpire for making calls they disagree with.

When you leave the field you can ask each other questions: Does winning really matter? Was the anger worth the effort? Did yelling at the ump solve anything? Aren't the kids more interested in getting popsicles after the game than being all-stars? With the big picture in mind, the outcome of a Little League game has no lasting value. Really!

As you read this you might be wondering, *How is this guy going to transition from baseball parents to a lesson on worship?* Here it is: As you move forward in your spiritual journey, you'll be placed in thousands of situations where you'll need to think through your words and actions. Will what I say, do, and think really matter? Will my frustrations today matter in the long run? Will my life honor God if I do this?

When your life is fully surrendered to God's ways, you consider questions like these because you want to be responsible with the time, talents, and treasures God has given you. At the end of your life (which seems so far away) you'll think back on your life. You want to be able to say, "God, I love you. I lived life to the fullest and to honor you." Consistent evaluation of your life will lead to a life well lived.

During this lesson you'll discuss what an awesome reward that kind of life will bring.

FELLOWSHIP: CONNECTING Your Heart to Others'

As your small group has been meeting to discuss what worship is all about, hopefully you've gained some insights, deepened your faith, and made some strong friendships.

1 What have been some of the highlights from your small group times as you've met to do these lessons together?

2 Your view of worship may have changed since you began this workbook. Refer back to the first question of this book on page 22. How would you describe worship now?

DISCIPLESHIP: GROWING to Be Like Jesus

Paul was one of the great heroes of the church. As a strong leader, pastor, and teacher, he was humble enough to listen to God. He wrote more than half of the New Testament and traveled all over the world to spread the good news. Bigger than his achievements was his heart for God. After many years of serving Jesus—often in the midst of terrible suffering—he looked back on his life and didn't express any regrets when it came to the most important thing: a life fully surrendered to God.

⁶For I am already being poured out like a drink offering, and the time has come for my departure. ⁷I have fought the good fight, I have finished the race, I have kept the

faith. ⁸Now there is in store for me the crown of righteous-ness, which the Lord, the righteous Judge, will award to me on that day—and not only to me, but also to all who have longed for his appearing.

—2 Timothy 4:6-8

Paul wrote this letter to Timothy, a younger believer Paul had mentored. Do you have a Timothy—a person you're influencing spiritually?

Paul says he's fought the good fight. How would you describe the "fights" you've recently fought? Would they be considered good from God's point of view?

How is the "race" word picture similar to the "journey" word picture we've been using in this book? How is it different?

What do you need to do now to ensure that you finish the race?

How does the promise of a reward in heaven make it easier to completely surrender your life to God today?

As you've learned, your worship of God is much more than singing or going to church. Worship is about the way you live. What would the people who know you best say about your faith and the way you live in light of that idea?

When you're looking back on your life, what would you like to be able to say about your faith? About the way you lived?

MINISTRY: SERVING Others in Love

Recently I was eating a bowl of warm chili and a chunk of cornbread on a cold, rainy day. As I took the large pot of chili out of the fridge, not only did I see more chili than I could eat in a week, but I remembered my conversation with Edward, a 14-year-old from Africa.

World Vision, a relief agency, invited Edward to visit churches and tell us about the AIDS epidemic in his country. His story gripped my heart, and I grieved for his people. The excess chili immediately made me think of the people in his village who have so much less and deal with so much more pain than I ever will.

I wonder why you and I are blessed with so much more than Edward. As we bathe in our abundance, Edward's friends are dying of AIDS and starving by the thousands. The experience brought me to my knees as I was overwhelmed with all the hurt and hopelessness in the world.

I don't tell you this so you'll feel guilty, but I do want to tell you about Edward so you can ask yourself some hard questions. The world has an overwhelming number of people in difficult circumstances. You can't help all of them, but you can help somebody.

Take a few minutes and write about how God might use your life to make a difference and reach others in Jesus' name. As you write, consider these ideas:

- Complete surrender of your life
- Life in America with its financial resources
- Evangelism
- Fighting the fight
- Finishing the race
- "From everyone who has been given much, much will be demanded; and from the one who has been entrusted with much, much more will be asked" (Luke 12:48).

What can your small group do to share some of your resources to minister to others less fortunate than you? (If you're struggling with this area, perhaps reading Matthew 25:40 will help.)

EVANGELISM: SHARING Your Story and God's Story

Who do you know who has spent his or her adult life sharing God's story?
- What makes that person attractive as a human being?

Is there more to the good fight and finishing the race than being evangelistic?
- If you were to spend the rest of your life sharing God's story and your story, would that be enough for you to say on your deathbed, "I have fought the good fight...I have finished the race"?

WORSHIP: SURRENDERING Your Life to Honor God

Where do you go from here? You could easily move into the next book in the LIFETOGETHER series and forget the progress you've made over the past six weeks. To prevent that from happening, make a commitment to one another within your small group to help and challenge each other to live lives surrendered to God and his ways.

Finish this sentence: **For me to worship with my entire life I need to...**
📖 Share what you wrote with your group.

14

Pray for one another and thank God for each person in your group.

15

WHAT'S NEXT?

16

Do you agree to continue meeting together? If yes, continue on with the remaining questions.

Five other books in the LifeTogether series help you establish God's purposes in your life. Discuss which topic your group will study next.

Starting to Go Where God Wants You to Be: 6 Small Group Sessions in Beginning Life Together

Connecting Your Heart to Others': 6 Small Group Sessions on Fellowship

Growing to Be Like Jesus: 6 Small Group Sessions on Discipleship

Serving Others in Love: 6 Small Group Sessions on Ministry

Sharing Your Story and God's Story: 6 Small Group Sessions on Evangelism

You might have noticed this study guide, **SURRENDERING Your Life to Honor God**, contained one session on each topic.

17 Turn to the **Small Group Covenant** (page 88). Do you want to change anything in your covenant—time, date, shared values, and so on? Write down the changes you agree upon. (Transfer them into your next LifeTogether book.)

18 This is a good time to make suggestions for other changes—starting **on time,** paying attention when others are sharing, rotating leadership responsibilities, or whatever ideas you have—for improving the group.

AT HOME THIS WEEK

Daily Bible Readings
Check out the Scriptures on page 104.

Memory Verses
Try memorizing a verse from page 108.

Journaling
Use **SCRIBBLE** pages, 113-125
- Write whatever is on your mind.
- Read your journal entry from last week and write a reflection on it.
- Respond to this question: *What will I have to do to get to the end of my life and be able to say. "I have fought the good fight, I have finished the race"?*

Wrap It Up
Write out your answers to the session questions your group didn't have time to discuss.

LEARN A LITTLE MORE

Drink offering
In Jewish customs, wine was poured on the altar or on an animal being sacrificed (see Genesis 35:14 and Exodus 29:41). Paul viewed his life as an offering that was surrendered to God and poured out in dedication.

Crown of righteousness
In Roman athletic games, a winner was given a crown, something like a gold medal

given at the Olympics. In this passage Paul wasn't referring to an earthly award but an eternal crown from the King of heaven. (See 2 Corinthians 5:10 and Matthew 19:27 for other verses about rewards.)

The righteous Judge

Paul wrote this letter while imprisoned in Rome. It wasn't the first time he went to jail because of his faith, but it appears that he knew it would be the last time. As he looked back on his life, he had few regrets. As he looked forward, his hope was in God, the one who will judge righteously. He would stand before a corrupt human judge, but Paul considered that a mere formality before being able to stand before the perfect Judge.

FOR FURTHER STUDY

Numbers 15:1-12
Philippians 1:12-26; 2:14-18

NOTES

If you are watching the LIFETOGETHER DVD, you may use this page to take notes.

NOTES

APPENDIXES

MY STORY

Jesus' life, death, and resurrection is the greatest story ever told. That's God's story.

The second greatest story ever told is how God has impacted your life—your testimony. Write your story here.

SMALL GROUP COVENANT

Read through the following covenant as a group. Discuss concerns and questions. You may modify the covenant based on the needs and concerns of your group members. Those who agree with the terms and are willing to commit themselves to the covenant as you've revised it should sign their own books and the books of everyone entering into the covenant.

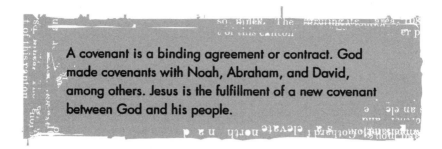

A covenant is a binding agreement or contract. God made covenants with Noah, Abraham, and David, among others. Jesus is the fulfillment of a new covenant between God and his people.

If you take your commitment to the Small Group Covenant seriously, you'll find that your group will go deep relationally. Without a covenant you may find yourselves meeting simply for the sake of meeting.

If your group decides to add some additional values (character traits such as be encouraging or be kind), write the new values at the bottom of the covenant page. Your group may also want to create some small group rules (actions such as not interrupting when someone else is speaking or sitting up instead of lying down). You can list those at the bottom of the covenant page also.

Reviewing your group's covenant, values, and rules before each meeting will become a significant part of your small group experience.

OUR COVENANT

I, _____ , as a member of our small group, acknowledge my need for meaningful relationships with other believers. I agree that this small group community exists to help me deepen my relationships with God, Christians, and other people in my life. I commit to the following:

Consistency I will give my best effort to attend every time our small group meets.

Honesty I will take risks to share truthfully about the personal issues in my life.

Confidentiality I will support the foundation of trust in our small group by not participating in gossip. I will not reveal personal information shared by others during our meetings.

Respect I will help create a safe environment for our small group members by listening carefully and not making fun of others.

Prayer I will make a committed effort to pray regularly for the people in our small group.

Accountability I will allow the people in my small group to hold me accountable for growing spiritually and living a life that honors God.

This covenant, signed by all the members in this group, reflects our commitment to one another.

Signature	Date
Signature	Date
Signature	Date
Signature	Date
Signature	Date
Signature	Date
Signature	Date
Signature	Date
Signature	Date
Signature	Date

SMALL GROUP Roster

name	EMAIL

SURRENDERING your life to honor God

Phone	Address	school & GRADE

HOW TO KEEP YOUR SMALL GROUP FROM BECOMING A CLIQUE

Cliques arise naturally because we all want to belong—God created us to be connected in community with one another. The same drive that creates community creates cliques. A clique isn't just a group of friends, but a group of friends uninterested in anyone outside the group. Cliques result in pain for those who are excluded.

If you reread the first paragraph of the introduction **"Read Me First"** (page 9), you see the words *spiritual community* used to describe your small group. If your small group becomes a clique, it's an *unspiritual* community. You have a clique when the biblical purpose of fellowship turns inward. That's ugly. It's the opposite of what God intended the body of Christ to be.

- Cliques make your youth ministry look bad.
- Cliques make your small group appear immature.
- Cliques hurt the feelings of excluded people.
- Cliques contradict the value God places on each person.
- Few things are as unappealing as a youth ministry filled with cliques.

Many leaders avoid using small groups as a means toward spiritual growth because they fear the groups will become cliquish. But when they're healthy, small groups can improve the well-being, friendliness, and depth of your youth ministry.

> Be wise in the way you act toward outsiders;
> make the most of every opportunity.
>
> —Colossians 4:5

Here are some ideas for preventing your small group from turning into a clique:

Be Aware

Learn to recognize when people feel like they don't fit in with your group. It's easy to forget when you're an insider how bad it feels to be an outsider.

Reach Out

Once you're aware of a person feeling left out, make efforts to be friendly. Smile, shake hands, say hello, ask them to sit with you or your group, and ask simple yet personalized questions. A person who feels like an outsider may come across as defensive, so be as accepting as possible.

Launch New Small Groups

Any small group that has the attitude of "us four and no more" has become a clique. A time will come when your small group should launch into multiple small groups if it gets too big. The bigger a small group gets, the less healthy it will become. If your small group understands this, there will be a culture of growth instead of cliques. New or introverted people often are affected by cliques because they have a hard time breaking through the existing connections that the small group members already have. When you start new groups you'll see fellowship move from ugly to what God intended—a practical extension of his love.

Challenge Others

Small group members expect adult leaders to confront them for acting like a clique. Instead of waiting for an adult to make the move, shock everyone by stepping up and challenging what you know is destructive. Take a risk. Be a spokesperson for your youth ministry and your student peers by leading the way—be part of a small group that isn't cliquey and one who isn't afraid to challenge the groups who are.

By practicing these key ideas, your group will excel at reaching out to others and deepening the biblical fellowship within your church.

ACCOUNTABILITY QUESTIONS

During your small group time, you'll have opportunities to connect with one other person in the group—your spiritual partner. Relationships can go deeper if you have the same partner for the entire book or even the entire LifeTogether series. Be as mellow as you want or crank it up to a higher level by talking throughout the week and checking in with each other about your spiritual journeys.

For those who want to go to a deeper level with their spiritual partners, here's a list of questions you can use as a guide for accountability. Depending on the time you have available, you might discuss all of them or only a couple.

The Wonder Question
Have you maintained an attitude of awe and wonder toward God?
(Have you minimized him? Placed him in a box? Forgotten to consider his character?)

The Priority Question
Have you maintained a personal devotional time (quiet time) with God?
(Have you allowed yourself to become too busy? Filled your life with too much activity?)

The Morality Question
Have you maintained integrity in the way you live?
(Have you compromised your integrity or the truth with your actions? Your thoughts? Your words?)

The Listening Question
Are you sensitive to the promptings and leading of the Holy Spirit?
(Have you drowned out his voice with too much noise?)

The Relationships Question

Have you maintained peaceful relationships and resolved conflicts to the best of your ability? (Have you caused conflict, offended others, or avoided resolving tension?)

The Prayer Question

How can I pray for you this week?

SPIRITUAL HEALTH assessment

Evaluating your spiritual journey is a good thing. Parts of your journey will take you to low spots, while others will lead you to high places. Spiritual growth is not a smooth incline—loopy roller coaster is more like it. When you regularly consider your life, you'll develop an awareness of God's Spirit working in you. Evaluate. Think. Learn. Grow.

The assessment in this section is a tool, not a test. The purpose of this tool is to help you evaluate where you're at in your faith journey. No one is perfect in this life, so don't worry about what score you get. It won't be published in your church bulletin. Be honest so you have an accurate idea of how you're doing.

When you finish, celebrate the areas where you're relatively healthy, and think about how you can use your strengths to help others on their spiritual journeys. Then think of ways your small group members can aid one another to improve weak areas through support and example.

 FELLOWSHIP: CONNECTING Your Heart to Others'

1. I meet consistently with a small group of Christians.

1	2	3	4	5
poor				outstanding

2. I'm connected to other Christians who hold me accountable.

1	2	3	4	5
poor				outstanding

3. I can talk with my small group leader when I need help, advice, or support.

1	2	3	4	5
poor				outstanding

4. My Christian friends are a significant source of strength and stability in my life.

1	2	3	4	5
poor				outstanding

5. I regularly pray for others in my small group between meetings.

1	2	3	4	5
poor				outstanding

6. I have resolved all conflicts I have had with other Christians and non–Christians.

1	2	3	4	5
poor				outstanding

7. I've done all I possibly can to be a good son or daughter and brother or sister.

1	2	3	4	5
poor				outstanding

Take time to answer the following questions to further evaluate your spiritual health (after your small group meets if you don't have time during the meeting). If you need help with this, schedule a time with your small group leader to talk about your spiritual health.

List the three most significant relationships you have right now. Why are these people important to you?

How would you describe the benefit you receive from being in fellowship with other Christians?

SURRENDERING your life to honor God

Do you have an accountability partner? If so, what have you been doing to hold each other accountable? If not, how can you get one?

DISCIPLESHIP: GROWING to Be Like Jesus

11. I have regular times of conversation with God.

1	2	3	4	5
poor				outstanding

12. I'm a closer friend with God this month than I was last month.

1	2	3	4	5
poor				outstanding

13. I'm making better decisions this month when compared to last month.

1	2	3	4	5
poor				outstanding

14. I regularly attend church services and grow spiritually as a result.

1	2	3	4	5
poor				outstanding

15. I consistently honor God with my finances through giving.

1	2	3	4	5
poor				outstanding

16. I regularly study the Bible on my own.

1	2	3	4	5
poor				outstanding

17. I regularly memorize Bible verses or passages.

1	2	3	4	5
poor				outstanding

Take time to answer the following questions to further evaluate your spiritual health (after your small group meets if you don't have time during the meeting). If you need help with this, schedule a time with your small group leader to talk about your spiritual health.

What books or chapters from the Bible have you read during the last month?

What has God been teaching you from Scripture lately?

What was the last verse you memorized? When did you memorize it? Describe the last time a memorized Bible verse helped you.

MINISTRY: SERVING Others in Love

21. I am currently serving in some ministry capacity.

1	2	3	4	5
poor				outstanding

22. I'm effectively ministering where I'm serving.

1	2	3	4	5
poor				outstanding

23. Generally I have a humble attitude when I serve others.

1	2	3	4	5
poor				outstanding

24. I understand God has created me as a unique individual and he has a special plan for my life.

1	2	3	4	5
poor				outstanding

25. When I help others, I typically don't look for anything in return.

1	2	3	4	5
poor				outstanding

26. My family and friends consider me to be generally unselfish.

1	2	3	4	5
poor				outstanding

27. I'm usually sensitive to the hurts of others and respond in a caring way.

1	2	3	4	5
poor				outstanding

Take time to answer the following questions to further evaluate your spiritual health (after your small group meets if you don't have time during the meeting). If you need help with this, schedule a time with your small group leader to talk about your spiritual health.

28 If you're currently serving in a ministry, why are you serving? If not, what's kept you from getting involved?

29 What spiritual lessons have you learned while serving?

30 What frustrations have you experienced as a result of serving?

EVANGELISM: SHARING Your Story and God's Story

31. I regularly pray for my non-Christian friends.

1	2	3	4	5
poor				outstanding

32. I invite my non-Christian friends to church.

1	2	3	4	5
poor				outstanding

33. I talk about my faith with others.

1	2	3	4	5
poor				outstanding

34. I pray for opportunities to share about what Jesus has done in my life.

1	2	3	4	5
poor				outstanding

35. People know I'm a Christian by more than my words.

1	2	3	4	5
poor				outstanding

36. I feel a strong compassion for non-Christians.

1	2	3	4	5
poor				outstanding

37. I have written out my testimony and am ready to share it.

1	2	3	4	5
poor				outstanding

Take time to answer the following questions to further evaluate your spiritual health (after your small group meets if you don't have time during the meeting). If you need help with this, schedule a time with your small group leader to talk about your spiritual health.

Describe any significant spiritual conversations you've had with unbelievers in the past month.

Has your faith been challenged by any non-Christians? If yes, how?

What have been some difficulties you've faced with sharing your faith?

What successes have you experienced recently in personal evangelism? (Success isn't limited to bringing people to salvation directly. Helping someone take a step closer at any point on his or her spiritual journey is success.)

WORSHIP: SURRENDERING Your Life to Honor God

42. I consistently participate in Sunday and midweek worship experiences at church.

1	2	3	4	5
poor				outstanding

43. My heart breaks over the things that break God's heart.

1	2	3	4	5
poor				outstanding

44. I regularly give thanks to God.

1	2	3	4	5
poor				outstanding

45. I'm living a life that, overall, honors God.

1	2	3	4	5
poor				outstanding

46. I have an attitude of wonder and awe toward God.

1	2	3	4	5
poor				outstanding

48. I use the free access I have into God's presence often.

1	2	3	4	5
poor				outstanding

Take time to answer the following questions to further evaluate your spiritual health (after your small group meets if you don't have time during the meeting). If you need help with this, schedule a time with your small group leader to talk about your spiritual health.

Make a list of your top five priorities. You can get a good idea of your priorities by evaluating how you spend your time. Be realistic and honest. Are your priorities in the right order? Do you need to get rid of some or add new priorities? (As a student you may have some limitations. This isn't ammo for dropping out of school or disobeying parents!)

50 List ten things you're thankful for.

51 What influences, directs, guides, or controls you the most?

DAILY BIBLE READINGS

A s you meet together with your small group friends for Bible study, prayer, and encouragement, you'll grow spiritually. No matter how deep your friendships go, you're not likely to be together for your entire lives, so you need to learn to grow spiritually on your own too. God has given you an incredible tool to help—his love letter, the Bible. The Bible reveals God's love for you and gives directions for living life to the fullest.

To help you, you'll find a collection of Bible passages that reinforce each week's lesson below. Every day *read* the daily verses, *reflect* on how the verses inspire or challenge you, and *respond* to God through prayer or by writing in your journal or on the journaling pages in this book.

Check off the passages as you read them. Don't feel guilty if you miss a daily reading. Simply do your best to develop the habit of being in God's Word daily.

☐ Week 1
Psalm 29
Psalm 96:1-9
Psalm 95
Isaiah 29:13-14
matthew 15:8-9

☐ Week 2
Psalm 100
Psalm 46:10
Psalm 150
Matthew 4:9-10
Hebrews 13:15

☐ Week 3
Isaiah 64:8
Isaiah 43:18-19
Romans 6:13
John 4:23-24
1 Corinthians 10:14-22

☐ Week 4
Jeremiah 29:11
Proverbs 19:21
Psalm 16:11
Proverbs 3:5-6
1 Corinthians 2:9

☐ Week 5
Matthew 5:6
Matthew 6:19-24
Matthew 6:33
Matthew 22:37-39
John 6:35

☐ Week 6
Colossians 1:10
Psalm 103:1-5
Romans 12:1-2
2 Chronicles 16:9
2 Corinthians 3:18

HOW TO STUDY THE BIBLE

The Bible is the foundation of all the books in the LIFETOGETHER series. Every lesson contains a passage from the Bible for your small group to study and apply. To maximize the impact of your small group experience, it's helpful if each participant spends time reading and studying the Bible during the week. When you read the Bible for yourself, you can have discussions based on what *you* know the Bible says instead of what another member has heard second- or third-hand about the Bible. You also minimize the risk of depending on your small group for all your Bible study time.

Growing Christians learn to study the Bible on their own so they can learn to grow on their own. Here are some principles about studying the Bible to help you give God's Word a central place in your life.

Choose a Time and Place

Since we're so easily distracted, pick a time when you're at your best. If you're a morning person, then give that time to study the Bible. Find a place away from phones, computers, and TVs, so you are less likely to be interrupted.

Begin with Prayer

Make an effort to acknowledge God's presence. Thank him for his gifts, confess your sins, and ask for his guidance and understanding as you study his love letter to you.

Start with Excitement

We easily take God's Word for granted and forget what an incredible gift we have. God wasn't forced to reach out to us, but he did. He's made it possible for us to know him, understand his directions, and be encouraged, all through the Bible. Remind yourself how amazing it is that God wants you to know him.

Read the Passage

After choosing a passage, read it several times. You might want to read it slowly, pausing after each sentence. If possible, read it out loud. Originally the Bible was heard, not read.

Keep a Journal

Respond to God's Word by writing down how you're challenged, truths you want to remember, thanksgiving and praise, sins to confess, commands to obey, or any other thoughts you have.

Dig Deep

When you read the Bible, look deeper than the plain meaning of the words. Here are a few ideas about what you might find.

Truth about God's character
What do the verses reveal about God's character?

Truth about your life and our world
You don't have to figure out life on your own. Life can be difficult, but when you know how the world works you can make good decisions guided by wisdom from God.

Truth about the world's past
The Bible reveals God's intervention in our mistakes and triumphs throughout history. The choices we read about—good and bad—serve as examples to challenge us to greater faith and obedience. (See Hebrews 11:1-12:1.)

Truth about our actions
God will never leave you stranded. Although he allows us to go through hard times, he is always with us. Our actions have consequences and rewards. Just like he does in Bible stories, God can use all of the consequences and rewards caused by our actions to help others.

As you read, ask these four questions to help you learn from the Bible:

> What do these verses teach me about who God is, how he acts, and how people respond?

- What does this passage teach about the nature of the world?
- What wisdom can I learn from what I read?
- How should I change my life because of what I learned from these verses?

Ask Questions

You may be tempted to skip over parts you don't understand, but don't give up too easily. Understanding the Bible can be hard work. If you come across a word you don't know, look it up in a regular dictionary or a Bible dictionary. If you come across a verse that seems to contradict another verse, see whether your Bible has any notes to explain it. Write down your questions and ask someone who has more knowledge about the Bible than you. Buy or borrow a study Bible or check the Internet. Try these sites to begin with:

www.twopaths.com
www.gotquestions.org
www.carm.org

Apply the Truth to Your Life

The Bible should make a difference in your life. It contains the help you need to live the life God intended. Knowledge of the Bible without personal obedience is worthless and causes hypocrisy and pride. Take time to consider the condition of your thinking, attitudes, and actions, and wonder about how God is working in you. Think about your life situation and how you can serve others better.

More Helpful Ideas

- Take the position that the times you have set aside for Bible reading and study are nonnegotiable. Don't let other activities squeeze Bible study time out of your schedule.
- Avoid the extremes of being ritualistic (reading a chapter just to mark it off a list) and lazy (giving up).
- Begin with realistic goals and boundaries for your study time. Five to seven minutes a day may be a challenge for you at the beginning.
- Be open to the leading and teaching of God's Spirit.
- Love God like he's your parent (or the parent you wish you had).

MEMORY VERSES

The word *memory* may cause some people to throw this book and kick the dog. Throughout your school years, you have to memorize dates, places, times, and outcomes. Now we're telling you to memorize the Bible?! Seriously?

Not the entire Bible. Start with some key verses. Here's why: Scripture memorization is a good habit for a growing Christian to develop. When God's Word is planted in your mind and heart, it has a way of influencing how you live. King David understood this when he wrote; " I have hidden your word in my heart that I might not sin against you" (Psalm 119:11).

Challenge one another in your small group to memorize the six verses below— one for each time your small group meets. Hold each other accountable by asking about one another's progress. Write the verses on index cards and keep them handy so you can learn and review them when you have free moments (standing in line, before class starts, when you've finished a test and others are still working, waiting for your dad to get out of the bathroom...). You'll be surprised at how many verses you can memorize as you work toward this goal and add verses to your list.

Week 1

> Therefore, I urge you, brothers,
> in view of God's mercy,
> to offer your bodies as living sacrifices,
> holy and pleasing to God—this is your
> spiritual act of worship.
> —Romans 12:1

Week 2

> Great is the Lord and most worthy of praise;
> his greatness no one can fathom.
> —Psalm 145:3

SURRENDERING your life to honor God

Week 3

Your eyes saw my unformed body.
All the days ordained for me were written
in your book before one of them came to be.

—Psalm 139:16

Week 4

And without faith it is impossible to
please God, because anyone who comes to him
must believe that he exists and that
he rewards those who eternally seek him.

—Hebrews 11:6

Week 5

But whatever was to my profit
I now consider loss
for the sake of Christ.

—Philippians 3:7

Week 6

Into your hands I commit my spirit;
redeem me, O Lord,
the God of truth.

—Psalm 31:5

JOURNALING: SNAPSHOTS OF YOUR HEART

I n the simplest terms, journaling is reflection with pen in hand. A growing life needs time to reflect, so several times throughout the book you're asked to reflect in writing and you always have a journaling option at the end of each session. Through these writing opportunities, you're getting a taste of what it means to journal.

When you take time to write reflections in a journal, you'll experience many benefits. A journal is more than a diary. It's a series of snapshots of your heart The goal of journaling is to slow down your life to capture some of the great, crazy, wonderful, chaotic, painful, encouraging, angering, confusing, joyful, and loving thoughts, feelings and ideas that enter your life. Writing in a journal can become a powerful habit when you reflect on your life and how God is working.

You'll find room to journal on the following pages.

Personal Insights

When confusion abounds in your life, disorderly thoughts and feelings can become like wild animals. They often loom just out of range, slightly out of focus, but never gone from your awareness. Putting these thoughts and feelings on paper is like corralling and domesticating the wild beasts. Then you can look at them, consider them, contemplate the reasons they were causing you pain, and learn from them.

Have you ever had trouble answering the question, "How do you feel?" Journaling compels you to become more specific with your generalized thoughts and feelings. This is not to suggest that a page full of words perfectly represents what's happening on the inside. That would be foolish. But journaling can move you closer to understanding more about yourself.

Reflection and Examination

With journaling, once you recognize what you're to write about, you can then consider its value. You can write about your feelings, your situations, how you responded to events. You can reflect and answer questions like these:

- Was that the right response?
- What were my other options?
- Did I lose control and act impulsively?
- If this happened again, should I do the same thing? Would I do the same thing?
- How can I be different as a result of this situation?

Spiritual Insights

One of the main goals of journaling is to learn new spiritual insights about God, yourself, and the world. When you take time to journal, you have the opportunity to pause and consider how God is working in your life and in the lives of those around you, so you don't miss the work he's accomplishing. And journaling helps you remember.

What to Write

There isn't one way to journal, no set number of times per week, no rules for the length of each journal entry. Figure out what works best for you. Get started with these options:

A letter or prayer to God
Many Christians struggle with maintaining a consistent prayer life. Writing out your prayers can help strengthen it. Begin with this question: *What do I want to tell God right now?*

A letter to or a conversation with another person
Sometimes conversations with others can be difficult because we're not sure what we ought to say. Have you ever walked away from an interaction and 20 minutes later think, *I should have said…?* Journaling conversations before they happen can help you think through the issues and be intentional in your interactions with others. As a result, you can feel confident as you begin your conversations because you've taken time to consider the issues.

Conflict and pain
You may find it helpful to write about your conflicts with others, especially those that take you by surprise. By journaling soon after, you can reflect

and learn from the conflicts. You'll be better prepared for the next time you face a similar situation. Conflicts are generally difficult to navigate. Thinking through the interactions typically yields helpful personal insights.

When you're experiencing pain is a good time to settle your thoughts and consider the nature of your feelings. The great thing about exploring your feelings is that you're only accountable to God. You don't have to worry about hurting anyone's feelings by what you write in your journal (if you keep it private).

Personal motivation

The Bible is clear regarding two heart truths:
- How you act is a reflection of who you are on the inside (Luke 6:45).
- You can take the right action for the wrong reason (James 4:3).

The condition of your heart is so important. Molding your motives to God's desire is central to being a follower of Christ. The Pharisees did many of the right things, but for the wrong reasons. Reflect on the *real* reasons you do what you do.

Personal Impact

Have you ever gone to bed thinking, *That was a mistake. I didn't intend for that to happen!*? Probably! No one is perfect. You can't predict all of the consequences of your actions. Reflecting on how your actions impact others will help you relate better to others.

God's work in your life

If you write in your journal in the evening, you can answer this question: *What did God teach me today?*

If you journal in the morning, you can answer this question: *God, what were you trying to teach me yesterday that I missed?* When you reflect on yesterday's events, you may find a common theme that God may have been weaving into your life during the day, one you missed because you were busy. When you see God's hand in your life, even a day later, you know God loves you and is guiding you.

Scripture

Journal about whatever you learn from the Bible. Rewrite a verse in your own words, or figure out how a passage is structured. Try to uncover the key truths from the verses and figure out how the verses apply to your life.

SCRIBBLES

SCRIBBLES

Genesis

SCRIBBLES

SCRIBBLES

SCRIBBLES

SCRIBBLES

SCRBBLES

finest

SCRIBBLES

JOURNALING page

the house that Jack
maiden all forlorn
...'s baby yet
...ered man who
...d the cat...

...bought from the rat
...lay in the house that

SCRIBBLES

SCRIBBLES

SCRIBBLES

PRAYING IN YOUR SMALL GROUP

As believers, we're called to support one another in prayer, and prayer should become a consistent part of creating a healthy small group.

One of the purposes of prayer is to align our hearts with God's. By doing this, we can more easily think his thoughts and feel his feelings—in our limited human way. Prayer shouldn't be a how-well-did-I-do performance or a self-conscious, put-on-the-spot task to fear. Your small group may need time to get comfortable with praying out loud. That's okay.

Follow Jesus' Example

When you do pray, silently or aloud, follow the practical, simple words of Jesus in Matthew 6.

Pray sincerely.

"And when you pray, do not be like the hypocrites, for they love to pray standing in the synagogues and on the street corners to be seen by men. I tell you the truth, they have received their reward in full."

—Matthew 6:5

In the Old Testament, God's people were disciplined prayer warriors. They developed specific prayers to use for every special occasion or need. They had prayers for light and darkness, prayers for fire and rain, prayers for good news and bad. They even had prayers for travel, holidays, holy days, and Sabbath days.

Every day the faithful would stop to pray at 9:00 A.M., noon, and 3:00 P.M., a sort of religious coffee break. Their ritual was impressive, to say the least, but being legalistic has its downside. The proud, self-righteous types would strategically plan their schedules to be in the middle of a crowd when it was time for prayer so everyone could hear them as they prayed loudly. You can see the problem. What was intended to promote spiritual passion became a drama for the crowd.

The Lord wants our prayers addressed to him alone. That seems obvious enough, yet how many of us pray more with the need to impress our listeners than to communicate with God? This is the problem if you're prideful like the Pharisees about the excellent quality of your prayers. But it can also be a problem if you're new to prayer and concerned that you don't know how to "pray right." Don't concern yourself with what others think; just talk to God as if you were sitting in a chair next to him.

Pray simply.

"And when you pray, do not keep on babbling like pagans, for they think they will be heard because of their many words. Do not be like them, for your Father knows what you need before you ask him."

—Matthew 6:7-8

The Lord doesn't ask to be dazzled with brilliantly crafted language. Nor is he impressed with lengthy monologues. It's freeing to know that he wants us to keep it simple.

Pray specifically.

"This, then, is how you should pray: 'Our Father in heaven, hallowed be your name, your kingdom come, your will be done on earth as it is in heaven. Give us today our daily bread. Forgive us our debts, as we also have forgiven our debtors. And lead us not into temptation, but deliver us from the evil one.'"

—Matthew 6:9-13

What the church has come to call **The Lord's Prayer** is a model of the kind of brief but specific prayers we may offer anytime, anywhere. Look at some of the specific items mentioned:

Adoration—hallowed be your name

Provision—your kingdom come...your will be done...give us today our daily bread

Forgiveness—forgive us our debts

Protection—lead us not into temptation

PRAYER REQUEST GUIDELINES

Because prayer time is so vital, small group members need to know some basic guidelines for sharing, handling, and praying for prayer requests. Without a commitment from each person to honor these simple suggestions, prayer time can be dominated by one person, be a gossipfest, or be a never-ending story time. (There are appropriate times to tell personal stories, but this may not be the best time.)

Here are a few suggestions for each group to consider:

Write the requests down.

Each small group member should write down every prayer request on the **Prayer Request Log** (pages 132-137). When you commit to a small group, you're agreeing to be part of the spiritual community, which includes praying for one another. By keeping track of prayer requests, you can be aware of how God answers them. You'll be amazed at God's power and faithfulness.

As an alternative, one person can record the requests and e-mail them to the rest of the group. If your group chooses this option, *safeguard confidentiality.* Be sure personal information isn't compromised. Some people share e-mail accounts with parents or siblings. Develop a workable plan for this option.

Give everyone an opportunity to share.

As a group, be mindful of the amount of time remaining and the number of people who still want to share. You won't be able to share every thought or detail about a situation.

Obviously if someone experiences a crisis, you may need to focus exclusively on that group member by giving him or her extended time and focused prayer. (However, *true* crises are infrequent.)

The leader can limit the time by making a comment such as one of the following:

- Everyone can share one praise or request.
- Simply tell us what to pray for. We can talk more later.
- We're only going to pray for requests about the people in our group.
- We've run out of time to share prayer requests. Take a moment to write down your prayer request and give it to me [or identify another person]. You'll get them by e-mail tomorrow.

Just as people are free to share, they're free to not share.

The goal of a healthy small group should be to create an environment where participants feel comfortable sharing about their lives. Still, not everyone needs to share each week. Here's what I tell my small group:

> As a small group we're here to support one another in prayer. This doesn't mean that everyone has to share something. In fact, I don't want you to think, *I've got to share something.* There's no need to make up prayer requests just to have something to say. If you have something you'd like the group to pray for, let us know. If not, that's fine too.

No gossip allowed.

Don't allow sharing prayer requests to become an excuse for gossip. This is easy to do if you all aren't careful. If you're not part of the problem or solution, consider the information gossip. Sharing the request without the story behind it helps prevent gossip. Also speak in general terms without giving names or details ("I have a friend who's in trouble. God knows who it is. Pray for me that I can be a good friend.").

If a prayer request starts going astray, someone should kindly intercede, perhaps with a question such as, "How can we pray for *you* in this situation?"

Don't give advice or try to fix the problem.

When people share their struggles and problems, a common response is to try to fix the problem by offering advice. At the right time, the group might provide input on a particular problem, but during prayer time, keep focused on praying for the need. Often God's best work in a person's life comes through times of struggle and pain.

Keep in touch.

Make sure you exchange phone numbers and emails before you leave the first meeting, so you can contact someone who needs prayer or encouragement before the next time your group meets. You can write each person's contact information on the **Small Group Roster** (page 90).

During the Small Group Gathering

- One person closes in prayer for the entire group.
- Pray silently. Have one person close the silent prayer time after a while with *Amen*.
- The leader or other group member prays out loud for each person in the group.
- Everyone prays for one request or person. This can be done randomly during prayer or, as the request is shared, a willing pray-er can announce, "I'll pray for that."
- Everyone who wants to pray takes a turn or two. Not everyone needs to pray out loud.
- Split the group into half and pray together in a smaller group.
- Pair up and pray for each other.
- On occasion, each person can share what he or she is thankful for before a prayer request, so prayer requests don't become negative from focusing only on problems. Prayer isn't just asking for stuff. It includes praising God and being thankful for his generosity toward us.

SURRENDERING *your life to honor God*

- If you're having an animated discussion about a Bible passage or a life situation, don't feel like you *must* cut it short for prayer requests. Use it as an opportunity to add a little variety to the prayer time by praying some *other* day between sessions.

Outside the Group Time

You can use these options if you run out of time to pray during the meeting or in addition to prayer during the meeting.

- Send prayer requests to each other via e-mail.
- Pick partners and phone each other.
- Have each person in the small group choose a day to pray for everyone in the group. Perhaps you can work it out to have each day of the week covered. Let participants report back at each meeting for accountability.
- Have each person pray for just one other person in the group for the entire week. (Everyone prays for the person on the left or on the right or draw names.)

PRAYER REQUEST LOG

DATE	who shared	ReQuest	rEsponse/ anSweR

PRAYER REQUEST LOG

DATE	who shared	ReQuest	r8sponse/anSweR

PRAYER REQUEST LOG

DATE	who shared	ReQuest	rEspOnse/ anSweR

PRAYER REQUEST LOG

DATE	who shared	ReQuest	r8sp0nse/ anSweR

PRAYER REQUEST LOG

DATE	who shared	ReQuest	rEsponse/ anSweR

PRAYER REQUEST LOG

DATE	who shared	ReQuest	rEsponse/ anSweR

LIFE TOGETHER FOR A YEAR

Your group will benefit the most if you work through the entire LIFETOGETHER series. The longer your group is together, the better your chances of maturing spiritually and integrating the biblical purposes into your life. Here's a plan to complete the series in one year.

I recommend you begin with **STARTING to Go Where God Wants You to Be**, because it contains an introduction to each of the five biblical purposes (though it isn't mandatory). You can use the rest of the books in any order.

As you look at your youth ministry calendar, you may want to use the books in the order they complement events the youth group will be participating in. For example, if you plan to have an evangelism outreach in the fall, study **SHARING Your Story and God's Story** first to build momentum. Study **SERVING Others in Love** in late winter to prepare for the spring break missions' trip.

Use your imagination to celebrate the completion of each book. Have a worship service, an outreach party, a service project, a fun night out, a meet-the-family dinner, or whatever else you can dream up.

SURRENDERING your life to honor God

Number of weeks	Meeting topic
1	Planning meeting—a casual gathering to get acquainted, discuss expectations, and refine the covenant (see page 88).
6	**STARTING to Go Where God Wants You to Be**
1	Celebration
6	**CONNECTING Your Heart to Others'**
1	Celebration
6	**SHARING Your Story and God's Story**
1	Celebration
6	**GROWING to Be Like Jesus**
1	Celebration
6	**SERVING Others in Love**
1	Celebration
6	**SURRENDERING Your Life to Honor God**
1	Celebration
2	Christmas break
1	Easter break
6	Summer break
52	One year

Dear Kathleen,

I just wanted to let you know how thankful I am for the dedication you showed me as my small group leader. I love telling people, "Kathleen is my small group leader — she's the best!" Next to God, you have had the greatest influence in my life. I want to grow up and love people like you, love Jesus like you do, love my future husband like you do, and be a small group leader like you.

What's amazing about you, is that all the girls in our small group felt like you liked them the most. We also felt your push. As I look back over my junior high and high school years, you loved me enough to challenge me to change. Thank you for always asking about my prayer life, my quiet times, my ministry, my heart. Thanks for seeing who I could be.

You've made a huge difference in my life. Thank you!

Love,
Sarah

Whether you are a student or a leader, when you're a part of a small group — investing your life in others — you're making a difference that will last an eternity. At Simply Youth Ministry we are dedicated to helping you do just that. For students, we've got tools like the *One Minute Bible*, that will help you grow in your faith. For leaders, we've got all kinds of resources that will help you simplify your ministry and save you time. For both of you, we have a deep appreciation for your commitment to serving Christ and loving each other.

doug fields'
simply youth ministry
simplifying ministry...saving you time.

toll free: 1-866-9-simply
simplyyouthministry.com

ABOUT THE AUTHORS

Doug Fields, a respected youth ministry leader for over two decades, has authored or coauthored more than 30 books, including **Purpose-Driven Youth Ministry, Your First Two Years of Youth Ministry,** and **Videos That Teach.** With an M.Div. from Fuller Theological Seminary, Doug is the youth pastor at Saddleback Church, president of simplyyouthministry.com, and a frequent presenter at Youth Specialties events. Doug and his wife, Cathy, have three children.

Brett Eastman is pastor of membership and small groups at Saddleback Church, where there are now over 1,500 small group leaders and a growing network of volunteer coaches and bivocational pastors. Brett created the Healthy Small Group strategy and he leads the Large Church Small Group Forums for the Leadership Network. Brett is coauthor of the DOING LIFE TOGETHER Bible study series. Brett and his wife, Dee, have five children.